The Loneliness Epidemic

Understanding and Overcoming the Modern Crisis of Social Isolation

Oliver Cook

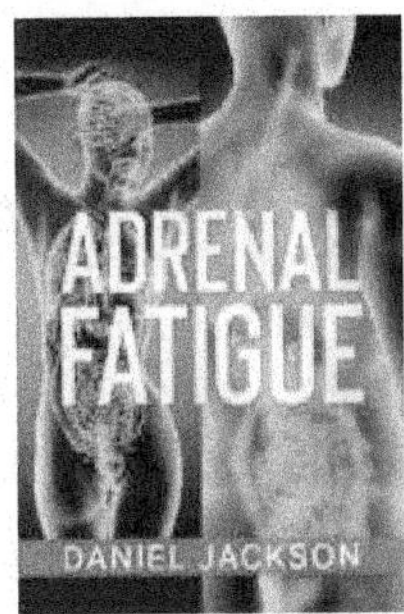

Take a look at more great books available from Rockwood Publishing

... some for FREE!

Just visit the link below:

rockwoodpublishing.co.uk

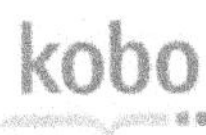

Contents

Introduction

The Silent Siren Call of Our Time: Unmasking Loneliness

Loneliness, often romanticized in literature and music, is a profound and deeply rooted social issue that has become a quiet epidemic of our time. We live in an era marked by extraordinary connectivity, yet paradoxically, we're witnessing a rise in the feelings of isolation and disconnection. This book seeks to delve into this enigma, to explore the roots and implications of this paradox and provide an understanding of the loneliness epidemic.

In this first chapter, we'll introduce the issue at hand and set the stage for the in-depth exploration that will follow in subsequent chapters. The topics we will cover include an overview of loneliness, a brief historical context, the understanding of loneliness in the psychological and social sciences, and the significance of addressing this issue.

Loneliness: A Universal Human Experience

Loneliness is an emotion intrinsic to our human experience. Everyone, regardless of age, race, or social status, can feel lonely. It is not merely a feeling of being alone, but a deeper sense of isolation, a disconnect from others, even when surrounded by people. Importantly, loneliness is subjective and varies greatly between individuals. For some, it might be an infrequent shadow that briefly passes over their life; for others, it's a constant, oppressive force.

Historically, loneliness has been a common topic in philosophy, literature, and the arts. From the Greek myth of Narcissus, who died from the sorrow of not being able to touch his reflection, to modern movies that showcase the lonely life of metropolitan individuals, loneliness has been a part of the human narrative. Yet, despite its prevalence in our stories, the understanding and the dialogue around loneliness remain surprisingly shallow.

Historical Context of Loneliness

In ancient times, humans lived in closely-knit communities where isolation was rare. Life revolved around communal activities, and the sense of belonging was profound. In modern times, however, the structure of society has changed dramatically. The focus has shifted from community living to individualism, and this shift has been accompanied by increased mobility, geographical dispersion, and a change in family dynamics. While these changes have brought freedom and opportunities, they have also led to a rise in social isolation and feelings of loneliness.

Loneliness in Psychology and Social Sciences

Psychologists and social scientists have dedicated significant efforts to studying loneliness. From a psychological perspective, loneliness has been linked to a range of mental health issues, including depression, anxiety, and lower self-esteem. In the realm of social sciences, the effects are seen in broader societal trends such as increased individualism, detachment from community involvement, and a general sense of social disconnect.

Why Addressing Loneliness Matters

Addressing loneliness is critical for both individual and societal wellbeing. On an individual level, chronic loneliness can lead to severe mental and physical health issues. It can increase the risk of heart disease, weaken the immune system, and even shorten life expectancy. On a societal level, loneliness can lead to social fragmentation and disintegration, affecting social cohesion and ultimately, the health of our communities and society as a whole.

In the subsequent chapters, we will delve into the causes, manifestations, and effects of loneliness, guided by research and scientific studies. We will explore potential solutions, drawing from psychology, sociology, and other fields, and discuss how we can collectively address the loneliness epidemic. It is through understanding and proactive measures that we can hope to mitigate this silent crisis and build a more connected, cohesive society.

Remember, in addressing this issue, we are not just countering a negative phenomenon but rather striving towards a positive one: the creation of a more empathetic, understanding, and connected society. So, let's embark on this journey of understanding the loneliness epidemic.

The Paradox of the Modern World

There is a powerful paradox in our modern world that bears repeating: in this age of hyperconnectivity, where we can instantly connect with anyone around the globe, feelings of loneliness and isolation are on the rise. As we delve deeper into the chapters of this book, we will unpack this paradox and explore the nuances that underpin it.

The internet, while revolutionizing communication, has also altered our social interactions in profound ways. While it allows us to maintain connections over vast distances, it can also create a veneer of connection that masks deeper feelings of isolation. There is a distinction between interacting in the digital sphere and sharing a physical space, experiencing mutual activities, or having face-to-face interactions. These layers of connection, often missing in our digital interactions, can contribute to a sense of loneliness even amid a bustling online social life.

The Role of Social and Political Sciences

Social and political sciences play an essential role in understanding the loneliness epidemic. They provide the tools to investigate the macro-level societal changes and political decisions that influence our sense of community, belonging, and, consequently, our experiences of loneliness. These disciplines help illuminate the societal norms, structures, and policies that may contribute to or alleviate loneliness, allowing us to better understand its root causes and devise effective strategies to address them.

The Journey Ahead

The journey that lies ahead in this book is as much about personal understanding as it is about societal change. It's about understanding our own experiences of loneliness and those of others around us. It's about recognizing how our societal structures, norms, and decisions influence our sense of connection. And it's about working towards creating a society that values and fosters genuine connections and community.

The loneliness epidemic may be a silent crisis, but it doesn't have to be a permanent one. By increasing our understanding, we can begin to address this issue, starting with ourselves and expanding outwards to our communities, our societies, and ultimately, our world.

This is our task and our journey. As we move forward in the chapters to come, we will explore loneliness in all its complexity, its causes and its effects, and most importantly, the ways we can overcome it. In doing so, we aim to bring light to the shadows of this silent epidemic and create a future where genuine connection and community thrive. We hope that you join us in this important endeavor.

Chapter 1: Defining the Loneliness Epidemic

The Modern Phenomenon: Social Isolation in a Connected World

Our journey begins by understanding what we mean by the 'loneliness epidemic'. The term 'epidemic' usually refers to the rapid spread of infectious diseases, but in recent years it has been extended to other social issues that have seen a rapid rise in prevalence, with loneliness being one of them. The loneliness epidemic is an urgent and growing issue, one that is entwined with the realities of the modern, technologically advanced world.

This chapter delves into the nature of this modern phenomenon. By understanding the nuances of social isolation in a connected world, we can start to understand how and why this paradox has taken hold and how it impacts our everyday lives.

The Digital Age and its Irony

The last few decades have witnessed an explosion of technological innovations that have transformed our lives in numerous ways. One of the most significant changes has been in how we communicate and connect with each other. Today, we live in a world where connecting with someone thousands of miles away is as simple as clicking a button.

We are more connected than ever before, but at the same time, research shows that we're also feeling more isolated. We live in an era of Facebook friends, Instagram likes, and Twitter followers. It's a world where the quantity of connections often outweighs the quality of those connections. We scroll through news feeds, liking and commenting on posts, but these interactions lack the depth and substance of face-to-face conversations. This superficial connectivity can often lead to a feeling of 'alone together'—being physically alone but digitally connected, fostering a sense of isolation despite the perceived connectedness.

The Deceptive Nature of Online Interactions

Online interactions, while convenient, often provide a distorted view of reality. Social media platforms are frequently a highlight reel of people's lives, showcasing their best moments and achievements. This can lead to comparison, envy, and a feeling of inadequacy, which can exacerbate feelings of loneliness.

Further, online interactions lack many elements inherent in face-to-face communication. The warmth of a smile, the comfort of a hug, or the empathy communicated through body language—these are absent in digital communication, and their absence can contribute to feelings of loneliness and disconnect.

The Changing Landscape of Community and Connection

The rise of individualism in the modern world has resulted in a shift from community-focused living to a more solitary existence. Increased mobility and flexibility in job markets mean people are moving more frequently, often leaving behind established social networks. Coupled with the reality of more single-person households, fewer community gathering spaces, and an overall decrease in community engagement, the opportunities for authentic, meaningful connections have decreased.

Our modern environments are also designed with less emphasis on social interaction. Urban planning often prioritizes efficiency and economy over communal spaces that encourage social interactions. This lack of shared spaces—combined with our fast-paced, busy lifestyles—limits our opportunities for spontaneous social encounters that could alleviate feelings of loneliness.

This modern reality has undoubtedly contributed to the loneliness epidemic, creating a society where we are physically close to each other yet emotionally distant. In this connected world, social isolation has become an unexpected outcome.

But understanding this is just the beginning. In the following chapters, we will dive deeper into the roots of the loneliness epidemic, studying the psychological, social, and political factors that have contributed to its rise.

Through this understanding, we aim to uncover pathways to address and ultimately overcome this modern crisis of social isolation. As we journey together, remember that each step we take towards understanding this issue is a step towards building a more connected, less lonely world.

Understanding Loneliness: A Psychological Perspective

Loneliness is not merely a by-product of our social lives, or lack thereof, but a complex psychological state that permeates our emotional well-being and mental health. To truly understand loneliness, we must delve into the human mind, drawing from decades of research in psychology and related disciplines. This chapter presents an in-depth exploration of loneliness from a psychological perspective, highlighting how our minds interpret, experience, and react to this pervasive emotion.

Loneliness and its Psychological Roots

The human mind is a social entity; we crave connection, understanding, and belonging. We are wired for social connection because, in prehistoric times, being part of a group was crucial for survival. This primal need has evolved over thousands of years into our modern psychological framework. When we perceive a deficit in our social connections, our mind interprets it as loneliness. Loneliness is subjective and deeply personal. Two people can have the same number of social contacts, yet one may feel lonely while the other does not. This difference lies in the quality, not the quantity, of these relationships. Loneliness arises when our actual social connections do not meet our desired connections. It's the perception of being alone that causes emotional distress, not the objective state of being alone.

Loneliness, Perception, and Cognition

Our perceptions and cognitions play a critical role in loneliness. It's our mind that interprets our social interactions, our relationships, and our place within our social networks. Cognitive theories of loneliness suggest that lonely individuals have a cognitive bias that distorts social situations.

Lonely individuals often perceive social situations more negatively, expect rejection, and are more likely to remember social interactions as less satisfying than they actually were. These cognitive distortions reinforce feelings of loneliness, leading to a cycle of negative thoughts and emotions. Over time, these negative thought patterns can lead to withdrawal and isolation, further exacerbating loneliness.

The Psychological Consequences of Loneliness

Loneliness does not exist in a vacuum; it has far-reaching psychological consequences that ripple through our mental and emotional health. Chronic loneliness is associated with higher levels of stress, depression, and anxiety. It can lead to a negative spiral of emotions, where the lonely individual continually dwells on negative experiences, further reinforcing their feelings of loneliness.

Moreover, loneliness can disrupt sleep patterns, leading to insomnia, and can even impact our cognitive functions, leading to reduced attention and memory. Furthermore, the stress resulting from chronic loneliness can activate our body's stress response, leading to adverse physical health outcomes, such as cardiovascular disease and a weakened immune system.

Loneliness is also a significant risk factor for mental health disorders. Numerous studies have linked chronic loneliness to major depressive disorder, generalized anxiety disorder, and substance use disorders. The link between loneliness and mental health underscores the urgent need to address and prevent loneliness.

Loneliness Across the Lifespan

Loneliness is not confined to a particular age group. It affects individuals across the lifespan, although its manifestation and triggers may differ. Children and adolescents might experience loneliness due to bullying or feeling left out by their peers. For young adults, the transition into college or the workforce might trigger feelings of loneliness. Older adults might experience loneliness due to the loss of a spouse or friends, or due to physical health issues that limit their social activities.

Importantly, the experience of loneliness can impact different age groups differently. For example, in older adults, loneliness has been linked to cognitive decline and dementia. For adolescents, loneliness can interfere with critical social and emotional development, leading to long-term mental health issues. Understanding the impact of loneliness across different age groups can guide interventions and prevention strategies.

The Role of Society and Culture

Psychological experiences, including loneliness, are shaped by societal and cultural factors. Cultural norms and expectations can impact how individuals interpret and experience loneliness. For instance, in cultures that highly value independence and self-reliance, loneliness might be stigmatized and perceived as a personal failure, thereby exacerbating its impact.

Society's influence also extends to the formation of our self-identity and our understanding of our place within our social networks. In societies where individuals often move for work or study, there's a higher likelihood of people losing their social connections, thereby increasing feelings of loneliness.

The Interplay of Personality and Loneliness

Personality traits significantly influence how we perceive, interpret, and respond to social situations. Certain personality characteristics, such as introversion, neuroticism, and low self-esteem, are associated with higher levels of loneliness. For example, introverts might have fewer social interactions, but that doesn't necessarily mean they feel lonely. However, if an introvert desires more social interaction than they're currently experiencing, it could lead to feelings of loneliness.

Similarly, individuals with high levels of neuroticism tend to experience negative emotions more frequently and intensely. They might perceive social situations more negatively, thereby experiencing higher levels of loneliness. People with low self-esteem might feel unworthy of love and connection, leading to self-imposed isolation and increased feelings of loneliness.

Understanding the complex interplay between personality and loneliness can help individuals and therapists target these traits through interventions such as cognitive-behavioral therapy, thereby reducing feelings of loneliness.

Loneliness: A Call to Action

The psychological perspective of loneliness paints a complex picture of interrelated cognitive, emotional, and behavioral factors. This complexity, however, should not deter us but rather inspire a call to action. By understanding how our mind processes loneliness, we can find ways to challenge our negative thought patterns, address our cognitive biases, and cultivate social skills that promote connection.

As we continue to explore loneliness in this book, remember that understanding is the first step towards change. Loneliness, while distressing, is a universal human experience, one that reminds us of our fundamental need for connection. By addressing it head-on, we can turn this crisis into an opportunity—an opportunity to build a society where no one feels alone, where every individual feels seen, heard, and valued. We hope you'll join us on this transformative journey.

Societal Implications of the Loneliness Epidemic

Just as loneliness can profoundly impact an individual's mental and physical health, it also reverberates through our societies, influencing everything from public health to the economy. In this chapter, we will explore the societal implications of the loneliness epidemic, drawing upon research from sociology, economics, and public health. This comprehensive exploration will highlight the magnitude and urgency of addressing loneliness at a societal level.

Loneliness and Public Health

Loneliness has substantial implications for public health. As previously discussed, chronic loneliness can lead to a host of mental and physical health problems, from cardiovascular disease to depression. These health outcomes not only affect individuals but also ripple through healthcare systems, impacting healthcare utilization, healthcare costs, and overall public health.

Increasingly, researchers and healthcare providers are recognizing loneliness as a social determinant of health, similar to poverty, education, and access to healthcare. Lonely individuals are more likely to visit the doctor, have higher utilization of emergency services, and have longer hospital stays. All these factors strain healthcare systems, increase healthcare costs, and draw resources away from other pressing health issues.

Additionally, loneliness can interfere with health behaviors. Lonely individuals are more likely to engage in health-damaging behaviors such as smoking, excessive alcohol consumption, and physical inactivity. These behaviors further exacerbate health disparities and contribute to poorer health outcomes at a population level.

Loneliness, Productivity, and the Economy

Beyond public health, the loneliness epidemic also has economic consequences. The impact of loneliness on mental and physical health can affect productivity and workforce participation. For example, employees who are lonely may have higher rates of absenteeism due to health problems related to loneliness. They may also have lower productivity due to the psychological distress associated with chronic loneliness.

Moreover, loneliness can affect job performance and job satisfaction. Lonely employees are less likely to be engaged at work, and they may experience lower job satisfaction, both of which can affect overall productivity. In a world where economies increasingly rely on innovation and collaboration, loneliness can hinder teamwork, creativity, and performance.

The economic impact of loneliness extends to caregiving and social services as well. Lonely individuals, particularly older adults, may require more assistance, whether from professional caregivers or social services. This increase in demand can strain these resources and lead to higher costs for both individuals and society.

The Social Fabric: Loneliness and Community

Loneliness doesn't only have implications for public health and the economy—it also affects the very fabric of our societies. It can erode community cohesion and contribute to a cycle of social disconnection. When individuals feel lonely, they're more likely to withdraw from their communities, leading to weaker social networks and less community engagement.

This loss of social cohesion can have far-reaching effects. Communities with strong social ties tend to have lower crime rates, better health outcomes, and higher levels of civic participation. They're also more resilient in the face of crises, from natural disasters to economic downturns.

On the other hand, communities marked by high levels of loneliness and social disconnection may face greater challenges in these areas.

Loneliness and Social Inequality

Finally, it's essential to note that loneliness is not evenly distributed in society. Certain groups are more likely to experience loneliness, including older adults, individuals with mental and physical health conditions, and marginalized populations. This uneven distribution of loneliness can exacerbate social inequalities and lead to further disparities in health, well-being, and economic opportunities.

For example, individuals with lower socioeconomic status may have fewer resources to combat loneliness, such as access to quality healthcare, recreational activities, or transportation to visit friends and family. Marginalized groups may experience loneliness due to discrimination, stigma, or lack of representation in their communities.

Towards a Connected Society

Understanding the societal implications of the loneliness epidemic underscores the urgency and necessity of addressing this issue on a systemic level. This isn't just a matter of enhancing individual well-being but also a crucial step towards healthier, more equitable, and more connected societies.

Addressing loneliness requires collective action across multiple sectors, including public health, education, business, and government. Public health campaigns can raise awareness about the health impacts of loneliness and promote strategies for social connection. Schools and universities can foster environments that encourage inclusivity and belonging, equipping young people with the social skills needed to form meaningful relationships.

Businesses and employers have a role to play as well. They can create workplace cultures that value connection and well-being, offering resources to help employees manage loneliness and stress. They can also implement flexible work policies that balance productivity with employees' need for work-life balance and social connection.

Government policies can also have a significant impact on loneliness. Investments in public spaces, community programs, and social services can create opportunities for social interaction and support. Policies can also address social inequalities that contribute to loneliness, ensuring all individuals have the resources and opportunities to lead connected, fulfilling lives.

The societal implications of the loneliness epidemic may seem daunting, but they also present an opportunity. They remind us that our social connections are not just a source of personal happiness but also a vital public resource.

They challenge us to reimagine our societies, to build communities that foster connection, and to create systems that prioritize well-being.

By addressing loneliness, we can create societies that are not just less lonely, but also healthier, more resilient, and more equitable. We hope you'll join us on this transformative journey.

Chapter 2: The Evolution of Social Connection

The Historical Human: Connection in Early Societies

To truly grasp the severity of the modern loneliness epidemic, it's instructive to trace back the roots of human social connection. Indeed, our evolution as a species is deeply intertwined with our ability to form complex social networks. A look back at early societies and our inherent social nature can offer insights into our modern struggle with social isolation and loneliness.

The Dawn of Social Connection: Survival and Evolution

The earliest human societies were centered around kinship and communal living, predicated on the principle that survival was contingent on cooperation. As the famed anthropologist Richard Leakey notes, "we are, at heart, a social species." Our ability to communicate, form relationships, and collaborate is believed to be the driving force behind our survival and growth as a species.

In hunter-gatherer societies, collaboration was not just beneficial; it was imperative for survival. Hunting required collective efforts, while gathering and sharing food resources promoted a more stable and sustainable lifestyle. These practices necessitated communication, relationship-building, and mutual reliance, creating an environment where strong social bonds were forged, maintained, and cherished.

The Role of Culture and Rituals

Culture and rituals also played an essential role in fostering social connection. Shared belief systems, values, and traditions cultivated a sense of belonging and unity among community members. Rituals, from shared meals to religious ceremonies, provided regular avenues for communal interactions, reinforcing social bonds and strengthening group cohesion.

Even in times of conflict, these bonds were a source of resilience. The shared experience of overcoming adversity often resulted in stronger community ties, fostering a sense of shared identity and collective strength.

From Nomadic to Settled Societies: The Impact on Social Connection

With the advent of agriculture around 10,000 years ago, human societies underwent a profound transformation. As communities transitioned from nomadic to settled lifestyles, social structures became more complex. Societies grew larger, which had both positive and negative implications for social connection.

On the one hand, settled societies could support larger populations, providing opportunities for more diverse and nuanced social interactions. On the other hand, as societies expanded, maintaining close connections with all members became more challenging. As a result, social hierarchies, divisions of labor, and class systems started to emerge, creating both physical and social distances among community members.

The development of writing and other forms of long-distance communication allowed societies to maintain connections over vast distances, but it also signaled a shift from face-to-face interaction to more impersonal forms of communication. This transition marked a pivotal moment in the evolution of human social connection, setting the stage for the ways we communicate and connect today.

The Historical Human in the Modern Age

Fast forward to our current age, and we find ourselves in societies that are larger and more complex than ever before. While our ability to connect has exponentially grown due to technological advancements, our societies often lack the close-knit community bonds that characterized our early history.

However, this historical perspective isn't intended to idealize past societies or downplay the significant challenges they faced. Instead, understanding our deep-rooted propensity for social connection can serve as a reminder of the inherent value we place on relationships, belonging, and community.

In the face of the modern loneliness epidemic, it encourages us to tap into our primal instincts for connection. It challenges us to reimagine our societies in a way that prioritizes meaningful social interactions, community engagement, and inclusivity, harking back to the communal spirit that carried our species through the ages.

As we explore the loneliness epidemic further in this book, we'll continually draw from this historical understanding. It will inform our examination of the impact of modern society on loneliness and guide our exploration of potential solutions. Above all else, it serves as a vital reminder that at our core, we are social beings, wired for connection and cooperation.

Shifting from Past to Present

As we shift our gaze from the past to the present, we begin to see more clearly how certain aspects of modern life contribute to feelings of loneliness and social isolation. We live in a time where communication is at our fingertips, yet meaningful connection often feels out of reach. We're part of vast social networks, yet we often feel unseen and unheard.

In upcoming chapters, we'll delve into how the rapid pace of technological advancements, changes in family structure, urbanization, and the rise of individualism contribute to our modern loneliness epidemic. We'll also examine how societal pressures, income inequality, and other social factors can lead to feelings of disconnection.

The Power of Looking Back

The value of this historical perspective lies in the fact that it allows us to imagine a different future. By understanding our innate capacity for connection and cooperation, we can seek ways to rebuild our communities and rekindle our sense of belonging. We can strive to create societies that nurture our natural propensity for connection, promoting wellbeing on an individual and societal level.

Our examination of early human societies also highlights the role of community and shared experiences in fostering connection. In a world where individual achievements are often celebrated over communal ones, there's a profound lesson in this: our strength and resilience lie not in isolation, but in our bonds with one another.

In the face of the loneliness epidemic, our historical human self reminds us of our fundamental need for social connection. It inspires us to foster a sense of belonging in our societies, cultivate shared experiences, and prioritize human connections over the convenience of technological interactions.

As we continue on this journey of understanding and addressing the loneliness epidemic, let's keep our historical human in mind. The lessons of the past can guide us in navigating the complexities of the present, empowering us to overcome the loneliness epidemic and build societies where everyone feels seen, heard, and deeply connected.

Industrial Revolution and Urbanization: Shifts in Social Constructs

The Industrial Revolution, a period that spanned the late 18th to early 19th centuries, was a defining moment in human history. It saw the shift from agrarian and handicraft economies towards mechanized production and industry. The implications of this revolution were far-reaching, influencing nearly every aspect of human life, including how we live, work, and connect with one another. The rise of factories and mechanized production led to unprecedented urbanization. People migrated from rural areas to burgeoning cities in search of jobs and better lives. As a result, cities swelled in size and number, becoming melting pots of different cultures, traditions, and socio-economic classes.

Crowded Cities, Isolated Lives

One might assume that densely populated cities would be the antidote to loneliness. Yet, paradoxically, these urban landscapes often fostered social isolation. People found themselves living amid thousands, even millions of others, yet feelings of disconnect were pervasive. How did this happen?

First, the nature of work changed dramatically. Pre-industrial societies were typically agrarian, with people working closely with family or community members. Work was tied to the rhythms of nature, and despite the hardships, it often engendered a sense of belonging and mutual reliance. However, in factories, work became mechanized and regimented, a far cry from the communal farming practices of the past.

Factory workers often worked long hours in harsh conditions, leaving little time or energy for socializing. Also, the nature of factory work often required a level of focus that discouraged conversation or camaraderie. Work shifted from being a collective effort to an individual endeavor, leading to a sense of isolation even in crowded factories.

The Fracturing of Traditional Support Networks

The mass migration to cities also meant that traditional support networks were fractured. Families were often split apart, with individuals or small family units moving to the city while others stayed behind in rural areas. In cities, people found themselves living among strangers, cut off from the familial and communal bonds that characterized rural life.

The urban living conditions didn't help either. Housing was often overcrowded, with multiple families sharing small spaces, leading to a lack of privacy and tensions among inhabitants. While there were undoubtedly opportunities for connection, the challenges of urban life often made it hard to form and maintain meaningful relationships.

The Rise of Individualism

The Industrial Revolution also saw the rise of individualism. Success was increasingly tied to individual effort and ambition, rather than communal achievement. This cultural shift further contributed to feelings of loneliness and isolation. As people were encouraged to focus on individual achievements, they were often left feeling disconnected from their communities.

Urbanization and Loneliness in the Modern Context

Fast forward to the present day, and many of the challenges first encountered during the Industrial Revolution still hold. Modern cities are bustling, dynamic spaces, yet they're also places where loneliness can easily take root.

People move frequently for jobs, often finding themselves in new cities or countries, away from their support networks. Urban life is fast-paced and competitive, leaving little time for leisure or socializing. The cultural focus on individual achievement is stronger than ever, often at the expense of community and connection.

Furthermore, modern urban environments are shaped by economic inequality, with stark divides between wealthy and impoverished neighborhoods. These disparities can lead to social isolation, as people from different socio-economic backgrounds often have limited interactions.

However, it's not all bleak. Cities also offer unique opportunities for connection. They're places of diversity and dynamism, where people from different walks of life can meet and interact. They house a multitude of social, cultural, and recreational venues that can facilitate social connections.

The challenge lies in leveraging these opportunities to combat loneliness and promote social connection. This involves creating inclusive, community-focused urban environments and fostering a culture that values connection and mutual support as much as individual achievement.

Lessons from the Past, Insights for the Future

Looking back at the Industrial Revolution and the onset of urbanization provides crucial insights into the loneliness epidemic. It demonstrates how large-scale societal changes can disrupt traditional social structures and norms, leading to increased feelings of social isolation.

More importantly, this historical perspective reveals the complex relationship between societal progress and social connection. While developments like the Industrial Revolution and urbanization have undoubtedly brought about significant advancements, they have also presented new challenges to maintaining social connections.

These lessons from the past can inform our response to the current loneliness epidemic. They underscore the importance of considering social implications when envisioning societal progress. They remind us of the value of community and the human need for connection, reinforcing the importance of these elements in our modern societies.

As we navigate the complexities of the 21st century, these insights can guide us in fostering societies that nurture social connections, despite the challenges posed by urbanization and modern life. They can encourage us to strive for progress that enhances human connection, rather than undermining it.

In the following chapters, we will explore how other societal shifts and technological advancements have influenced the loneliness epidemic. We will delve into the role of the digital age, exploring how the advent of social media and virtual communication channels have influenced our social connections.

As we examine these factors, our understanding of the historical human and the social shifts induced by the

Industrial Revolution will continue to inform our perspective. The goal is to leverage this understanding to not just analyze the problem but to envision a future where social connection is prioritized and loneliness is effectively addressed. It's a challenging task, but by drawing on the lessons of the past, we can strive to create societies that nurture our inherent need for connection and belonging, ultimately overcoming the modern crisis of social isolation.

The Rise of Digitalization: From Physical to Virtual Socialization

As we navigate further into the 21st century, one of the most defining shifts in our society has been the rise of digitalization. In the span of a few decades, we've transitioned from a world connected through landline telephones and letters to one intricately linked through digital networks.

The rapid advance of technology has reshaped how we communicate, work, learn, and socialize. Today, we're part of vast, interconnected digital networks that span continents, making it possible to communicate instantly with someone thousands of miles away. This transformation has brought unprecedented opportunities, but it has also presented new challenges for maintaining social connection. Let's delve deeper.

A New Realm of Connectivity

The digital realm offers myriad ways for us to connect. We can maintain long-distance friendships, participate in global communities centered around shared interests, or engage in lively debates with strangers. Theoretically, we should never feel alone.

Platforms like Facebook, Instagram, and Twitter, alongside messaging apps like WhatsApp and WeChat, allow us to keep in touch with friends, family, and acquaintances. Meanwhile, online forums, interest-based communities, and social networking sites bring together people from diverse backgrounds, fostering interaction and exchange of ideas.

Furthermore, digitalization has enriched our means of communication. We're not just limited to words; we can use images, videos, GIFs, and emojis, adding depth and nuance to our online conversations.

From Physical to Virtual: The Shift in Socialization

With all these possibilities for connection, socialization has increasingly moved from the physical to the virtual realm. This shift has significant implications.

Physical social interactions are multi-sensory experiences, filled with non-verbal cues like body language, tone of voice, and facial expressions. These cues enrich our interactions, fostering empathy and understanding. In the digital realm, these elements are often missing or significantly diminished. The subtleties of face-to-face communication can get lost, leading to misunderstandings and feelings of disconnect.

Moreover, while online platforms allow us to connect with a broad network of people, they can also foster superficial interactions. The constant stream of status updates, pictures, and posts encourages us to share and consume content quickly, often at the expense of meaningful dialogue.

The Paradox of Digital Connectivity

What emerges from this landscape is a curious paradox: we're more connected than ever, yet loneliness persists. A tweet, a status update, or a text message can't replace the experience of shared laughter, a comforting hug, or a sympathetic ear. Our digital connections, as extensive as they might be, can't always fulfill our need for deep, meaningful social interaction.

Moreover, the online world can often become a space of comparison and competition, further exacerbating feelings of isolation. The carefully curated lives we see on social media can lead to feelings of inadequacy, as we compare our ordinary lives to the highlight reels of others.

Maintaining a Healthy Balance

In the face of this digital paradox, it's essential to maintain a healthy balance between our online and offline social lives. Online connections can supplement but should not replace face-to-face interactions. It's also crucial to foster meaningful interactions online, focusing on quality over quantity.

As a society, we need to acknowledge and address the potential downsides of digitalization while leveraging its benefits. Digital tools can be incredibly useful in combating loneliness, particularly for those who may have limited opportunities for face-to-face interaction, such as the elderly, individuals with disabilities, or those living in remote areas. The key lies in using these tools to foster meaningful connections, not just passive interaction.

Embracing Digitalization Mindfully

The rise of digitalization represents a profound shift in our social landscape. As we move from physical to virtual socialization, we must navigate this new terrain with care, understanding, and a commitment to maintaining meaningful social connections.

Let's embrace the connectivity that digitalization offers, but do so mindfully. This means acknowledging the limitations of digital communication and striving for balance. It means fostering an online culture that values depth and authenticity over superficial engagement. It means leveraging digital tools to enhance, not replace, our face-to-face interactions.

Moreover, as the digital landscape continues to evolve, it's crucial to keep the conversation going. Let's continually assess how changes in technology are affecting our social connections. Let's innovate, experiment, and strive to create a digital world that nurtures our inherent need for meaningful social interaction.

This is a grand challenge, but it's one we must undertake. By embracing digitalization mindfully, we can leverage the vast potential of the digital world to combat loneliness and foster connection, helping to overcome the modern crisis of social isolation. As we navigate this path, let's remember that at the core of our hyper-connected digital world, it's the human-to-human connections that truly matter.

Ultimately, our journey through the rise of digitalization reaffirms a core truth: Our need for connection is as essential as it was in the early days of our species. It has survived the transformative forces of the Industrial Revolution and urbanization, and it persists in the digital age.

By acknowledging and nurturing this innate need, we can chart a course towards a future where connection thrives, and loneliness is effectively addressed.

The road is complex, but with insight, creativity, and collective action, it's a journey we can embark on, one step, one interaction, and one connection at a time.

Chapter 3: Technological Influences and the Paradox of the Digital Age

Social Media and Loneliness: A Paradox of Connection and Disconnection

The advent of social media has revolutionized our world, transforming how we interact, share information, and engage with our surroundings. Platforms like Facebook, Twitter, Instagram, and Snapchat, among others, have not only served as tools of communication but also as vast social landscapes where we can express ourselves, build relationships, and engage with communities.

These platforms promise an end to isolation, a world where everyone is connected. Yet, it's within this hyper-connected digital world that many of us grapple with profound loneliness, a paradox that merits in-depth exploration.

The Social Media Landscape: A Web of Connections

In the realm of social media, we are never alone. We have followers and friends, likes and comments, shares and retweets. We are part of multiple groups, communities, and networks. We share our thoughts, experiences, triumphs, and failures. We engage in dialogues, debates, and discussions. It's a bustling digital society where everyone has a voice.

In essence, social media creates an intricate web of connections, linking us to others across geographical boundaries and cultural divides. We can connect with friends from the past, build relationships with people across the globe, and engage with communities that share our interests and passions.

The Paradox of Social Media: Connection and Disconnection

While social media connects us in unprecedented ways, it's also here, within this web of connections, that feelings of loneliness often emerge. The very platforms that promise to end isolation can inadvertently foster feelings of disconnection and inadequacy.

The virtual world of social media is, in many ways, a highlight reel of people's lives. We see the successes, the celebrations, and the joyous moments. However, we seldom see the struggles, the mundane, the ordinary. This selective sharing can create unrealistic expectations and feelings of inadequacy. When we compare our everyday lives with the curated highlights of others, it can lead to a sense of isolation.

Additionally, the nature of communication on social media can often be superficial. We engage in 'liking', 'sharing', and 'commenting', but these interactions often lack the depth and nuance of face-to-face communication. While we're 'connected' to hundreds or even thousands of people, these connections can sometimes feel hollow and unfulfilling.

The Implications: Understanding and Addressing the Paradox

The paradox of social media – the coexistence of connection and disconnection – is an essential component of the loneliness epidemic. As we grapple with feelings of loneliness within our digital landscapes, we must strive to understand and address this paradox.

One approach is to promote authentic, meaningful engagement on social media. Encouraging deeper conversations, sharing not just our triumphs but also our struggles, and focusing on the quality of connections rather than the quantity can help alleviate feelings of loneliness. Furthermore, we must balance our online interactions with face-to-face social activities. While social media can supplement our social lives, it's not a replacement for real-world interactions. Ensuring we spend time with others in person can help us maintain a healthy social balance.

Finally, we must address the social comparison and feelings of inadequacy that social media can foster. This involves promoting a culture of authenticity and self-compassion, where we acknowledge that everyone has struggles, and it's okay not to be perfect.

Navigating the Social Media Paradox

The role of social media in the loneliness epidemic represents a complex paradox. On one hand, it offers unprecedented opportunities for connection. On the other, it can inadvertently foster disconnection and loneliness.

Ultimately, as we navigate this paradox of connection and disconnection, our goal is to chart a course that leverages the connective potential of social media while mitigating its loneliness-enhancing pitfalls.

The task is undeniably complex, but by taking a thoughtful, evidence-based approach, we can leverage the power of social media to help, rather than hinder, our quest to overcome the loneliness epidemic. Together, we can unravel the paradox and chart a path towards a digitally connected world that fosters authentic, meaningful social interactions, helping us combat the crisis of social isolation in our modern world.

The Impact of Digital Overload on Loneliness

In the previous sections, we've explored the paradox of social media and the subtle ways in which our interconnected digital world can leave us feeling isolated.

However, there's another facet of our digital landscape that contributes significantly to the loneliness epidemic, which is digital overload. This refers to the feeling of being overwhelmed by the volume and pace of digital information we consume, as well as the continual demands for our online attention.

The Digital Deluge: Information, Distraction, and Overwhelm

We live in an era of information abundance. From the moment we wake up to the time we go to sleep, we're inundated with emails, social media updates, news alerts, messages, and notifications. Our devices buzz and beep, drawing our attention to the ceaseless flow of digital content. Our screens light up with new information even as we struggle to digest what we've already consumed.

This digital deluge can lead to a state of constant distraction where our attention is perpetually divided. We're concurrently present in our physical surroundings and the digital world, navigating both simultaneously. The result is that we're often not fully present in either.

The cognitive toll of this digital overload is significant. It can lead to fatigue, stress, and a diminished capacity to focus. But what does this mean for loneliness?

Digital Overload and Loneliness: Disconnected in a World of Connections

At first glance, it may seem counterintuitive to link digital overload with loneliness. After all, isn't all this information and connectivity a means to keep us more intertwined with the world around us? Ironically, the opposite often proves true.

Firstly, digital overload can lead to a sense of social exhaustion. As we try to keep up with our various social media feeds, respond to messages, and engage with online communities, the sheer volume of social information can be overwhelming. The more overwhelmed we feel, the less capacity we have for meaningful engagement, leading to shallow, surface-level interactions that do little to alleviate feelings of loneliness.

Secondly, the state of constant distraction caused by digital overload can make it difficult for us to be fully present during our offline social interactions. We've all witnessed scenes where people sit together, each engrossed in their digital devices, physically present but socially disconnected. This divided attention can diminish the quality of our face-to-face social interactions, leaving us feeling lonely even in the company of others.

Finally, the always-on nature of digital connectivity can blur the boundaries between work and personal time, between public and private space. This can lead to a sense of social pressure to be continually available and responsive, leaving little room for solitude, rest, and reflection, all of which are essential for our mental well-being and social resilience.

Navigating Digital Overload: Creating Spaces for Connection

Addressing the impact of digital overload on loneliness requires conscious effort at both individual and societal levels. We need strategies to manage our digital consumption, preserve our attention, and create spaces for meaningful connection.

At an individual level, this might involve setting boundaries for digital use. It could mean designating certain times as 'digital-free', turning off non-essential notifications, or practicing 'single-tasking' to preserve our attention. Cultivating practices of mindfulness can also help, encouraging us to be fully present in our interactions, both online and offline.

At a societal level, we need to foster a culture that recognizes and respects the need for digital boundaries. This could involve challenging the expectation of constant availability, promoting digital wellbeing in schools and workplaces, and advocating for technology design that respects our attention rather than exploiting it.

Conclusion: Finding Balance in a Digital World

Digital overload is an inherent challenge in our information-saturated world, and its implications for loneliness are significant. It can lead to social exhaustion, distract us from our offline interactions, and erode the boundaries we need for personal well-being.

However, it's important to remember that digital technology is not inherently harmful. It is a tool, and like any tool, its impact depends on how we use it. We need to learn to wield this tool effectively, to reap the benefits of digital connectivity without succumbing to the pitfalls of digital overload.

This is not a straightforward task, nor is it a one-size-fits-all solution. Each of us has different needs and capacities when it comes to digital engagement. What works for one person might not work for another. The key is to cultivate a sense of digital self-awareness, understanding our own digital habits, how they impact us, and how we can align them with our wellbeing goals.

Digital technology has the potential to both isolate us and bring us together. It's a paradox we need to navigate as we strive to understand and overcome the loneliness epidemic in our modern world. By addressing digital overload, we can create a digital environment that fosters genuine connection, alleviates loneliness, and contributes to our overall wellbeing.

The loneliness epidemic is a pressing issue in our society, and its links with our digital lives are intricate and profound. By understanding these links, we can take positive steps towards addressing this crisis, forging a path towards a more connected, less lonely future.

So, as we continue this exploration, let's keep the conversation going. Let's keep questioning, learning, and connecting, both online and offline, as we navigate this complex digital world together.

Emerging Technology: VR, AR and AI's Role in Addressing Loneliness

In the preceding sections, we explored the nuances of our existing digital environment and its role in the loneliness epidemic. However, the technological landscape is ever-evolving, constantly unveiling new platforms and capabilities that can reshape our social connections. Three of the most significant emerging technologies are Virtual Reality (VR), Augmented Reality (AR), and Artificial Intelligence (AI). These technologies hold immense potential for addressing loneliness, but they also present new challenges that we need to navigate.

Virtual Reality (VR): Stepping into Shared Virtual Spaces

VR technology allows users to immerse themselves in a computer-generated world, experiencing a sense of 'presence' as though they were physically in that space. This capability offers novel opportunities for social connection. In a VR environment, users can meet, communicate, and engage in shared activities with others, regardless of their physical location. They can explore new worlds together, collaborate in virtual workspaces, or simply hang out in virtual social spaces.

For those grappling with loneliness, these shared virtual experiences can provide a sense of belonging and camaraderie. Moreover, VR can be particularly beneficial for those who face physical barriers to social interaction, such as those living with disabilities or residing in remote areas. By bridging the physical divide, VR can facilitate social interactions that may otherwise be impossible.

However, like any technology, VR also poses potential challenges. The immersive nature of VR can blur the line between the virtual and the real, potentially leading to disconnection from our physical surroundings. Additionally, while VR can facilitate social interaction, it does not automatically lead to meaningful connection. Creating virtual spaces that foster genuine social bonding, rather than mere novelty or entertainment, is a challenge that needs to be addressed as VR technology matures.

Augmented Reality (AR): Blending the Physical and the Digital

AR is another emerging technology that has the potential to reshape our social landscape. Unlike VR, which immerses users in a wholly digital environment, AR overlays digital elements onto our physical environment. This blend of the physical and the digital can enrich our social interactions, adding a new dimension to the way we connect with others.

For instance, AR can enhance our shared experiences by adding a layer of digital interaction to our physical social gatherings. It can also foster new forms of social connection by creating shared digital-physical spaces, such as AR games that bring people together in physical locations.

At the same time, the convergence of the digital and physical worlds that AR entails can create new forms of digital overload. As our physical spaces become infused with digital elements, we need to ensure that this digital layer enhances, rather than detracts from, our social connections.

Artificial Intelligence (AI): Simulating and Facilitating Social Connection

AI technology, particularly in the form of conversational AI or 'chatbots', presents another avenue for addressing loneliness. These AI systems can simulate human conversation, providing a form of social interaction for those who may lack other social outlets.

Moreover, AI can also facilitate human-to-human connection. For instance, AI algorithms can match individuals with similar interests, schedule social activities, or provide nudges to encourage social interaction. These tools can help individuals build and maintain their social networks, contributing to a sense of community and belonging.

Yet, AI also brings its own set of challenges. While AI can simulate conversation, it cannot replicate the emotional depth and complexity of human interaction. Relying on AI for social connection can thus lead to a form of 'pseudo-social' interaction that lacks the emotional richness of genuine human connection. Furthermore, issues of data privacy and algorithmic bias are significant concerns in the use of AI for social facilitation.

Navigating the Future: Balancing Potential and Pitfalls

Emerging technologies like VR, AR, and AI hold incredible potential for combating the loneliness epidemic, creating new avenues for connection and engagement. They can make our interactions more immersive, enrich our physical environment with digital elements, and even simulate or facilitate social engagement.

However, these technologies are not silver bullets. They carry their own set of challenges that we must grapple with. How do we ensure VR environments foster meaningful connection? How do we prevent AR from becoming another source of digital overload? How do we address the limitations and ethical concerns of AI-driven social interaction?

To harness these technologies effectively, we need to balance their potential with their pitfalls. We need to create guidelines and best practices for their use, grounded in our understanding of human psychology and social needs. We need to consider their impact on our social lives holistically, considering both their immediate effects and their broader implications.

We also need to remain adaptable. The landscape of technology is dynamic, with new platforms and capabilities emerging all the time. As these changes unfold, our understanding of their social implications will need to evolve as well. We need to stay attuned to these developments, continuing the conversation about how technology can contribute to a more connected, less lonely world.

In the end, our goal is not to simply adopt the latest technology, but to use it in a way that truly enhances our social wellbeing. This means not only leveraging the capabilities of these technologies but also addressing their limitations and challenges. It means understanding and respecting our social needs, and ensuring that our use of technology aligns with these needs.

The exploration of VR, AR, and AI's role in addressing loneliness opens up an exciting new frontier in our fight against the loneliness epidemic. As we continue this journey, let's approach these technologies with curiosity, caution, and an unwavering commitment to enhancing our social connections. In doing so, we can create a digital future that is not just technologically advanced, but also socially enriching.

Chapter 4: Societal and Economic Factors

Modern Work Structures and Isolation

The modern working environment has dramatically evolved in recent decades, fueled by technological advancements, economic shifts, and changes in societal norms. While these transformations have created numerous opportunities, they've also brought about new challenges, with isolation and loneliness becoming an increasing concern in modern work structures.

The nature of work has shifted from physically clustered, communal activities to more atomized, individualistic tasks, often involving digital technology. A trend towards more flexible, remote work, accelerated by the COVID-19 pandemic, has added to this sense of isolation for many. As we delve into the topic, we will discuss the causes of work-related loneliness, its implications, and how we can address this issue effectively, providing practical solutions to make the modern work environment less isolating.

The Isolating Nature of Modern Work Structures

The digital revolution has reshaped work in profound ways. Tasks that once required face-to-face interaction can now be completed from virtually anywhere. The rise of the gig economy, characterized by freelance, contract, and part-time work, further magnifies this isolation. Many workers operate independently, interacting with their employers, clients, or colleagues mostly through digital platforms.

Moreover, the recent pandemic has necessitated remote work for many sectors, limiting opportunities for personal connection that physical workplaces provide. Despite the convenience and flexibility offered, remote work can sometimes lead to a sense of detachment and isolation, as workers miss out on the incidental social interactions that offices provide.

Implications of Work-Related Isolation

The implications of work-related isolation are significant, both for individuals and organizations. Loneliness can adversely affect mental health, leading to increased stress, anxiety, and depression. It can also impact physical health, as research has linked chronic loneliness to a range of health conditions, including heart disease and weakened immune response.

From an organizational perspective, loneliness can undermine productivity, creativity, and job satisfaction. It can also hinder the sense of belonging and commitment to the organization, affecting employee retention and engagement.

Addressing Isolation in the Modern Work Structure

While the modern work structure has its challenges, there are also a variety of ways to address work-related isolation. Here are a few solutions that organizations, managers, and individuals can implement.

1. **Fostering a culture of connection**: Organizations can cultivate a culture that values social interaction and mutual support. This might include initiatives such as regular virtual team meetings, peer mentoring programs, and team-building activities.
2. **Effective use of technology**: While technology can contribute to isolation, it can also be part of the solution. Tools for instant messaging, video conferencing, and collaborative work can help maintain a sense of connection among remote workers.
3. **Flexible work arrangements**: Balancing remote and on-site work can help. Allowing employees some time in a shared physical workspace can offer opportunities for social interaction while still providing the benefits of flexibility.
4. **Wellbeing support**: Organizations can provide resources to support the mental health and wellbeing of their employees, such as counselling services, wellness programs, and mindfulness resources.

5. **Personal strategies**: On an individual level, strategies such as establishing a daily routine, taking regular breaks, and setting boundaries between work and personal life can help mitigate feelings of loneliness.

Modern work structures do present challenges to our innate need for connection. Yet, with awareness, strategic efforts, and adaptive use of technology, we can create work environments that promote social connection and reduce loneliness. In the next part of this chapter, we will explore another critical societal factor contributing to loneliness - urbanization and the resultant anonymity. We will continue to provide insights and offer solutions, building a comprehensive understanding of the loneliness epidemic and how to overcome it.

The Role of Housing and Urban Planning

The role of urban planning and housing is often understated when we discuss social isolation and loneliness. The design of our physical environment influences the way we interact with each other, impacting our sense of community, our access to social resources, and our feelings of loneliness. Urban planning decisions, including the design and allocation of residential areas, parks, public spaces, and transportation systems, can either foster social connection or exacerbate feelings of isolation.

The Connection Between Urban Design and Loneliness

Modern cities, with their densely packed high-rises and sprawling suburbs, often prioritize efficiency and economic productivity over human-scale design and community interaction. The design of housing and neighborhoods can inadvertently promote isolation.

Single-family homes separated by fences, high-rise apartments with little shared space, and suburbs with limited walkability all discourage spontaneous social interaction. This design orientation aligns with a societal emphasis on privacy and independence but comes at the cost of community connection.

Moreover, our cities and neighborhoods often lack adequate community spaces. Parks, community centers, cafes, and other public spaces play a critical role in facilitating social interaction. In their absence, opportunities for unplanned encounters - a conversation at the park, a chat at the local café - are lost.

Implications of Urban Isolation

Living in isolating urban environments can have profound impacts on mental and physical health. Research links loneliness with a range of health issues, from heart disease to depression. Moreover, living in an environment that discourages social interaction can lead to a diminished sense of belonging and community, further fueling feelings of loneliness.

Building Connection Through Urban Planning

Despite the challenges, the good news is that with thoughtful urban planning and design, we can create environments that foster social connection and help mitigate loneliness. Here are some strategies and solutions to consider:

1. **Promoting mixed-use developments**: Mixed-use developments that combine residential, commercial, and recreational spaces encourage people to live, work, and play in the same area. This approach increases the opportunity for social interaction, helping to build a sense of community.
2. **Creating inclusive public spaces**: Public spaces, such as parks, squares, and community centers, provide venues for social interaction. Inclusive design that caters to all ages and abilities can make these spaces more engaging and welcoming, encouraging use.
3. **Designing for walkability**: Neighborhoods that are easy to navigate on foot encourage residents to walk more and use communal spaces, increasing opportunities for social interaction. This might involve creating pedestrian-friendly streets, improving street lighting, or designing engaging street fronts.

4. **Fostering community through housing design**: Housing design can either promote or discourage social interaction. Shared spaces in apartment complexes, porches in suburban houses, and communal gardens can all encourage interaction among residents.

5. **Prioritizing affordable and diverse housing**: Ensuring a mix of housing types and price points can help create diverse, inclusive communities where people of different ages, family types, and income levels live together. This diversity can foster a richer community life.

The Role of Individuals and Communities

While urban planning plays a critical role, individuals and communities also have agency in shaping their social environments. Here are some ways people can foster connection within their urban environments:

1. **Participating in community activities**: Participating in local events, joining community organizations, or volunteering locally can foster a sense of belonging and reduce feelings of loneliness.

2. **Creating micro-communities**: This can be as simple as setting up a communal garden in your apartment complex, starting a neighborhood book club, or organizing a regular potluck dinner.

3. **Advocating for inclusive urban planning**: Citizens can play a role in shaping their cities by participating in local government and advocating for policies that promote social connection.

In conclusion, thoughtful urban planning and housing design have a significant role to play in combating the loneliness epidemic. By building our cities and neighborhoods in ways that encourage community interaction, we can make them more livable, vibrant, and mentally healthier places. From designing walkable streets to fostering diverse and inclusive communities, these strategies offer a proactive approach to addressing social isolation.

However, it's also important to remember that the built environment is just one piece of the puzzle. Personal commitment to community engagement, policies that address broader socioeconomic inequalities contributing to loneliness, and programs that provide mental health support are equally crucial to creating a society where everyone feels connected and valued.

The idea is to reframe our view of what a city could be. Not merely an assemblage of infrastructure, but a facilitator of human connection, interaction, and mutual support. In our rush to progress, we've constructed environments that, while efficient, overlook our basic human need to connect. It's time we address this oversight and place human connectivity at the forefront of our urban planning agenda.

Because at the end of the day, we are not solitary creatures. We are social beings, wired to connect. Our cities, our neighborhoods, and our homes should reflect this truth. Only then can we truly begin to address the loneliness epidemic and foster a more connected, less lonely world.

Remember, your home, your neighborhood, and your city are not just places. They are living, breathing entities that shape your interactions, your opportunities, and your experiences. It's time to shape them in ways that foster connection, not isolation, and ensure that no one, regardless of their circumstances, has to face the debilitating impact of loneliness.

And, while we navigate this path, it's crucial to remember that it's okay to seek help if you're feeling lonely. Reach out to friends, family, or professional help. You're not alone. With collective effort, we can overcome this modern crisis of social isolation, transforming our cities and societies into vibrant spaces of connectivity, community, and care.

Economic Inequality and Loneliness

The social fabric of our societies is intertwined with our economic realities in profound ways. Inequality, the gap between the rich and the poor, has become an inescapable reality of our time. However, economic inequality isn't just about uneven distribution of wealth or resources—it shapes our experiences, perceptions, and our emotional landscape, including feelings of loneliness and isolation.

It is essential to understand the nuanced relationship between economic inequality and loneliness to form effective strategies to address this modern-day epidemic. This chapter will delve deeper into the intersection between these two phenomena, offering practical solutions and strategies for individuals and communities alike.

The Psychological Impact of Economic Inequality

Economic inequality doesn't just separate people into different income brackets. It has the potential to segregate society into different realms of experiences, opportunities, and, ultimately, different levels of social connectivity. Research suggests that people from lower socioeconomic backgrounds often report higher levels of loneliness.

These feelings of loneliness may emerge for several reasons. One is the social divide: economic inequality can lead to divided social circles, where the haves and have-nots move in fundamentally different spheres of society, with little overlap or interaction. This segregation can create an 'us versus them' mentality that is fertile ground for feelings of social disconnection and loneliness.

The second, more subtle reason, is the psychological burden of inequality. Being on the lower rungs of the economic ladder can lead to feelings of inferiority, embarrassment, and social inadequacy. For some, it could mean declining invitations to social events due to the fear of not being able to afford it. For others, it might mean feeling out of place in social gatherings due to differences in lifestyle, experiences, or cultural capital.

This combination of social division and personal distress can lead to self-imposed social isolation, where people withdraw from social interaction to avoid the discomfort of these economic disparities. Thus, the specter of economic inequality extends its reach into our lives, not only through material scarcity but also through fostering a sense of social isolation and loneliness.

Bridging the Gap: Addressing Loneliness in the Face of Economic Inequality

So, how do we address loneliness in a world marked by growing economic inequality? We must approach this challenge from various angles, at both individual and systemic levels.

Empowering Communities:

First, we must invest in community initiatives and social infrastructure that fosters social inclusion. Libraries, community centers, public parks, and other inclusive spaces can facilitate interaction and connection among people from diverse economic backgrounds. These spaces offer opportunities for people to meet, interact, and form relationships based on shared interests or experiences, rather than their economic status.

Economic Policy:
Next, we need economic policies that directly address inequality. It's vital to promote equitable access to resources and opportunities, from education and healthcare to affordable housing. Reductions in income inequality, through policy measures such as progressive taxation, increased minimum wages, or enhanced social security nets, can alleviate the social divide and help to reduce feelings of loneliness.

Promoting Mental Health:
The link between economic inequality and loneliness underscores the need to consider mental health as a significant aspect of our public health approach. Investing in mental health resources, such as counselling and support groups, can provide vital lifelines for those struggling with loneliness. Furthermore, destigmatizing mental health can encourage more people to seek the help they need.

Personal Resilience:
On a personal level, developing resilience can also be a crucial tool in mitigating the impact of economic inequality on loneliness. Resilience, in this context, refers to the ability to maintain mental well-being in the face of adversity. This might involve learning coping mechanisms, such as mindfulness or cognitive behavioral techniques.

Addressing Loneliness Through Social Interventions:

In addition to personal resilience, there are social interventions that can make a difference. For instance, social programs that facilitate connections between different socio-economic groups can help to break down barriers and reduce feelings of isolation. Examples include mentoring programs, community service initiatives, and cultural exchange programs. Such interventions can provide shared experiences and common ground that help bridge the economic divide.

Improving Access to Technology:

In the digital age, access to technology can play a significant role in combating loneliness. However, the digital divide, which is often a reflection of economic inequality, can exacerbate feelings of isolation. Efforts to improve digital literacy and provide affordable access to technology can help those in economically disadvantaged situations to connect with others and access online resources that could mitigate feelings of loneliness.

Prioritizing Inclusive Design in Urban Planning:

Finally, it's essential to consider the role of urban planning in fostering or mitigating loneliness. High-density living, without adequately designed social spaces, can paradoxically increase feelings of isolation. In contrast, neighborhoods designed with inclusive social spaces – parks, community gardens, and communal facilities – can offer opportunities for social interaction and connection.

Efforts to incorporate such features into both existing and new urban environments can be a powerful way to mitigate the loneliness epidemic.

Economic inequality can exacerbate feelings of loneliness by creating both physical and psychological barriers to social connection. However, by understanding this relationship, we can begin to devise strategies and interventions at multiple levels to combat loneliness, even in the face of economic inequality. It's a complex issue, and no single solution will be a panacea. But with a multi-faceted approach, we can make significant strides towards creating a more socially connected and less lonely society, regardless of economic disparities.

Public Health Consequences of Loneliness

Loneliness does not merely cause emotional distress; it also has significant implications for public health. It has been linked to a range of health problems, including mental health issues like depression and anxiety, physical health conditions like heart disease and stroke, and even increased mortality rates.

Mental Health Consequences:
One of the most immediate consequences of chronic loneliness is its impact on mental health. Individuals experiencing persistent loneliness often report higher levels of depressive symptoms. The constant feelings of isolation can lead to a deep-seated feeling of sadness, a

hallmark of depression. Anxiety, too, is commonly seen in those who experience loneliness. This might present as generalized anxiety disorder, panic disorder, or other anxiety-related conditions.

Moreover, loneliness can contribute to more severe mental health disorders. Research has demonstrated that loneliness is a risk factor for the development of schizophrenia and other psychotic disorders. A study conducted by Matthew H. State, a psychiatrist at the University of California, San Francisco, found that adolescents who reported high levels of loneliness had a significantly higher risk of developing psychosis in adulthood.

Additionally, loneliness can exacerbate the symptoms of pre-existing mental health conditions. For those with bipolar disorder, periods of loneliness can trigger depressive episodes. For individuals with schizophrenia, feelings of isolation can intensify symptoms and lead to a worsening of their condition.

Physical Health Consequences:
The impact of loneliness extends beyond mental health and can profoundly affect physical health. A 2015 meta-analysis published in the journal Perspectives on Psychological Science found that loneliness and social isolation were associated with a significantly increased risk of premature death.

Loneliness has been linked with cardiovascular problems, including hypertension and heart disease. This is believed to be because chronic loneliness can lead to physiological changes, such as increased cortisol levels, that put stress on the heart.

Moreover, loneliness can also weaken the immune system, making individuals more susceptible to a variety of illnesses and diseases. Research from the University of Chicago found that loneliness can disrupt the production of white blood cells, essential for fighting off infections and disease.

Another significant physical health consequence of loneliness is its impact on sleep. Those who are lonely often report poor quality sleep, including difficulty falling asleep, frequent awakenings during the night, and feeling tired upon waking. Poor sleep quality, in turn, has been linked to a host of health problems, including obesity, diabetes, and cardiovascular disease.

Solutions and Mitigation Strategies:
Understanding the public health consequences of loneliness underscores the need for comprehensive, multi-level interventions.

Promoting Social Connections:
At a societal level, promoting social connections and community participation can be an effective way to reduce loneliness. This can be achieved through community

events, volunteering opportunities, social clubs, or other activities that encourage social interaction.

Access to Mental Health Services:

Increasing access to mental health services is also critical, given the strong link between loneliness and mental health issues. This could involve expanding public mental health programs, increasing funding for mental health research, and reducing the stigma associated with seeking help for mental health problems.

Building Resilience:

At an individual level, building resilience can also be beneficial. This can involve learning strategies to cope with stress, such as mindfulness and cognitive-behavioral techniques, and developing a strong social support network. In addition, physical exercise, a balanced diet, and adequate sleep can improve an individual's overall health and well-being and may help mitigate the physical health consequences of loneliness.

The public health implications of loneliness are vast and significant. Addressing this "epidemic of loneliness" requires a broad, multi-faceted approach that recognizes and addresses the multifaceted nature of loneliness and its numerous public health consequences.

Chapter 5: Psychological and Biological Factors

The Neuroscience of Loneliness: An Overview

Loneliness is not a mere state of mind or a passing feeling, rather it's an intricate interplay of psychological processes and biological systems that deeply affect our overall health and well-being. It's crucial to understand the neuroscience behind loneliness to appreciate how pervasive its impact can be and how we can employ science-backed strategies to combat it.

To begin with, our brains are wired for social connection. It's rooted in our evolutionary past where being part of a group increased chances of survival, and isolation was a serious threat. Thus, our brains developed mechanisms to detect and respond to social isolation. Today, that translates into what we know as feelings of loneliness.

Psychological Processes

Psychologically, feelings of loneliness can trigger cognitive processes that reinforce the sense of isolation. One such process is known as 'negative cognitive bias,' where lonely individuals tend to perceive social interactions more negatively and are more likely to interpret ambiguous social cues as threats or rejections. This can lead to self-fulfilling prophecies where people, feeling isolated, push others away, further increasing their sense of loneliness.

Biological Factors

The biological impact of loneliness is profound. When we're lonely, our bodies perceive it as a threat, leading to a 'fight or flight' response. This can result in increased levels of stress hormones like cortisol. Over time, persistently high cortisol levels can lead to a host of health issues, including heart disease, diabetes, and weakened immune system.

Research by neuroscientist John T. Cacioppo has highlighted how loneliness can affect the brain's structure and functionality. Chronic loneliness can alter the production and reception of neurotransmitters, the chemicals that allow neurons to communicate. It can affect dopamine and serotonin levels, two neurotransmitters essential to our feeling of happiness and well-being.

Neuroimaging studies have shown that feelings of social isolation can impact areas of the brain involved in cognition and affect, like the prefrontal cortex and the amygdala. The former is associated with decision-making and social behavior, and the latter plays a key role in emotional reactions.

Addressing Loneliness: The Neuroscience Perspective

Understanding the neuroscience of loneliness isn't merely an academic exercise—it provides us with concrete paths to address loneliness at its roots.

Therapeutic Interventions

Therapeutic interventions such as Cognitive Behavioral Therapy (CBT) can be particularly effective in tackling loneliness. CBT can help individuals identify and challenge negative cognitive biases, thereby altering their perception of social interactions. It's a tool to break the self-fulfilling prophecy of loneliness.

Social Connection

In terms of biological factors, one of the most effective ways to combat loneliness is through genuine social connection. Engaging in meaningful social activities can lead to the release of oxytocin, a hormone that promotes feelings of trust and bonding, and endorphins, the body's natural painkillers and mood elevators.

Mindfulness and Meditation

Practices like mindfulness and meditation have been shown to affect brain structure and function positively. They can help regulate stress response, reduce cortisol levels, and even enhance areas of the brain associated with empathy and emotional regulation.

Physical Activity

Regular physical activity is another practical way to mitigate the impacts of loneliness. Exercise triggers the release of endorphins and serotonin, promoting feelings of well-being and happiness. It can also offer opportunities for social interaction and community building.

The neuroscience of loneliness paints a picture of an intricate system where our brains, bodies, and social world interact. It's clear that loneliness is not a superficial issue but a deep-rooted condition that can have serious psychological and biological impacts. But with this knowledge comes the power to tackle it in a targeted and effective way.

Technology and Socialization

In our modern age, technology plays a significant role in addressing loneliness. Virtual Reality (VR) and Augmented Reality (AR) are emerging as potential tools to simulate social situations, providing realistic social interactions for those struggling with isolation.

While technology can never replace the need for genuine human connection, these digital tools can be a useful supplement, especially for those who, due to physical or mental health issues, may find traditional socializing challenging. For instance, VR has been successfully used in therapy to treat conditions like Post-Traumatic Stress Disorder (PTSD) and phobias, and its application to loneliness could be similarly beneficial.

Nutrition and Well-being

Lastly, our diet and nutrition can have a surprising influence on our mental state, including feelings of loneliness. The gut-brain axis is a term used to describe the bidirectional communication between the gut and the brain, which occurs via multiple pathways that include hormonal, neural, and immune mediators. The bacteria in our gut, known as the gut microbiome, can influence our brain's health and, consequently, our mood and mental state.

Ensuring a diet rich in probiotics and prebiotics, for instance, can help maintain a healthy gut microbiome, which is linked with better mental health outcomes. Omega-3 fatty acids, found in fish, flaxseeds, and chia seeds, are also known to have mood-enhancing properties. Thus, maintaining a balanced diet can be a vital part of the overall strategy to combat loneliness.

From a neuroscience perspective, loneliness is a complex and multifaceted issue that requires an equally complex and comprehensive response. We need to address it on multiple fronts, considering both our psychological and biological needs.

By understanding how our brain responds to social isolation, we can employ targeted interventions, from therapeutic techniques like CBT to daily practices like exercise and mindfulness. Utilizing emerging technologies can provide innovative solutions, and even our diet can play a role in maintaining our mental well-being.

Ultimately, the neuroscience of loneliness underscores the fundamental human need for connection. As social beings, our health and happiness are intrinsically tied to our relationships with others. And while the modern world may pose new challenges to social connection, with an understanding of our brain's workings, we are well-equipped to navigate these challenges and foster a sense of belonging and community.

Loneliness and Mental Health: Anxiety, Depression, and Beyond

Loneliness, the subjective feeling of social isolation, doesn't discriminate. Its clutches are felt across all ages, cultures, and socioeconomic groups. A modern crisis with a historical presence, loneliness has been linked to a plethora of mental health issues, ranging from anxiety and depression to more severe conditions like dementia. Understanding the association between loneliness and these mental health conditions is essential for devising effective strategies to manage and mitigate loneliness and its debilitating effects.

Loneliness and Anxiety

Anxiety, a common mental health disorder, is characterized by feelings of worry, unease, or fear that can be mild or severe. Its connection with loneliness is well-documented. When we feel socially isolated, our brain perceives it as a threat. Our biological defense mechanisms, honed through millions of years of evolution, kick in, triggering the 'fight or flight' response. This response, though beneficial in short-term threatening situations, can be detrimental when sustained over a long period, leading to heightened feelings of anxiety.

Loneliness can lead to a heightened state of sensitivity, where we are overly alert to potential social threats and more likely to perceive social interactions negatively. This can create a vicious cycle - our anxiety makes us withdraw from social situations, leading to greater loneliness, which in turn fuels our anxiety.

Solutions to Anxiety-Induced Loneliness

Cognitive-behavioral therapy (CBT) is a powerful tool to break this cycle. It allows us to challenge our negative thought patterns, helping us to view our social interactions in a more positive light, and thus, feel less isolated. Mindfulness techniques can also help manage anxiety by grounding us in the present and stopping us from ruminating on past social experiences or worrying about future ones.

Creating small, manageable social goals can also be effective. This could be something as simple as starting a conversation with a barista or joining a local club. These small victories can help build confidence and reduce anxiety associated with social interactions.

Loneliness and Depression

The link between loneliness and depression is robust. A meta-analysis of studies found that loneliness increases the risk of depression significantly. Loneliness can lead to feelings of worthlessness, hopelessness, and a lack of enjoyment in things once found pleasurable - all hallmark symptoms of depression.

One of the reasons loneliness can lead to depression is due to the impact of chronic loneliness on our brain. It can lead to increased inflammation and decreased production of new neurons in areas of the brain responsible for memory and emotion, such as the hippocampus, which can lead to depressive symptoms.

Solutions to Depression-Induced Loneliness

Depression is a serious mental illness that requires professional help. Treatment typically involves a combination of psychotherapy, medication, and lifestyle changes. In terms of loneliness, reconnecting with others is vital. This could involve reaching out to loved ones or seeking new social connections through clubs or online communities.

Therapeutic interventions such as interpersonal therapy (IPT), which focuses on improving the quality of one's relationships, can be beneficial. Furthermore, engaging in regular physical activity has been shown to be effective in alleviating depressive symptoms. Physical activity increases the production of endorphins, known as 'feel good' hormones, and promotes neural growth and new activity patterns in the brain that promote feelings of calm and well-being.

Loneliness and Other Mental Health Conditions

Beyond anxiety and depression, loneliness has been linked to more severe mental health conditions. Research shows loneliness can be a risk factor for conditions such as Alzheimer's disease and can exacerbate symptoms of conditions like schizophrenia.

The association between loneliness and mental health is complex and multifaceted. The strategies discussed are not exhaustive or universally applicable, but provide a starting point in addressing the complex relationship between loneliness and mental health. The mental health impacts of loneliness are a critical aspect of the loneliness epidemic, and it's vital to not only understand these connections but actively seek interventions that could help alleviate the suffering caused by loneliness.

If you find yourself in the grips of loneliness-induced mental health issues, it is essential to seek professional help. Licensed therapists and counselors are equipped with the knowledge and tools to help manage these conditions and guide you towards a healthier mental state. Moreover, they can provide resources and strategies to navigate social situations and cultivate meaningful relationships, thereby addressing the core issue of loneliness.

The advent of teletherapy and online counseling platforms has made mental health resources more accessible than ever. This is particularly beneficial for individuals who may feel anxious about face-to-face interactions or those who may not have readily available mental health resources in their immediate area.

In terms of societal changes, increasing mental health literacy is critical. There still exists a stigma around mental health, which can make individuals reluctant to seek help. Creating a society that understands, accepts, and supports mental health issues can encourage those suffering to reach out and find the help they need.

For people with severe mental health conditions like dementia and schizophrenia, specialized care may be necessary. Caregiving support, both professional and familial, plays a vital role in managing these conditions. Regular social interaction and stimulation are crucial for these individuals, and maintaining an environment conducive to this can significantly improve their quality of life.

Finally, the development and implementation of public policies to promote social inclusion and cohesion can help to tackle loneliness on a broader scale. For instance, urban planning can encourage social interaction by creating shared spaces like parks and community centers. Similarly, policies that foster economic equity can help mitigate loneliness induced by economic inequality.

The relationship between loneliness and mental health is complex, but by no means insurmountable. With the right support, strategies, and societal change, we can hope to see a decline in the loneliness epidemic and its associated mental health impacts. As a society, we must acknowledge the vital importance of social connections for our mental well-being and strive towards creating a world where no one has to suffer the pain of feeling socially isolated.

New Research: The Gut-Brain Axis and Its Influence on Social Behavior

In recent years, an exciting field of research has gained momentum: the gut-brain axis, the bidirectional communication between the gut and the brain. Emerging research is now linking this gut-brain interaction to a range of psychological and physiological health outcomes, including loneliness and social behavior.

It's easy to assume that our brains are the sole controllers of our feelings, thoughts, and behavior, including our social interactions. However, this is far from the complete picture. Our bodies are a complex system, where numerous parts work in conjunction, influencing each other. Among these, the relationship between our gut, often called the "second brain," and our actual brain, is increasingly gaining attention from the scientific community.

Our gut, with its network of neurons and production of neurotransmitters, closely interacts with the brain through a complex system involving the vagus nerve, immune system, and the endocrine (hormonal) system. This interaction is known as the gut-brain axis. The gut microbiota, the diverse community of microorganisms living in our gut, plays an essential role in this axis. Fascinatingly, research is starting to reveal how this gut microbiota can influence our brain and behavior, including social interaction.

Some compelling studies on animal models have shown that changes in gut microbiota can influence behavior. For example, germ-free mice, which are raised without any gut microbiota, have been found to display abnormal social behavior and increased anxiety-like behavior. When their guts are colonized with bacteria from normal mice, their behavior becomes more typical. Similar studies have also shown that administering certain types of probiotics can reduce stress-related behavior and improve mood.

In humans, the research is still in early stages, but the findings are promising. Some studies have found correlations between the diversity and types of gut bacteria and mental health conditions, including depression and anxiety. Further, there's preliminary evidence suggesting that modifying the gut microbiota through diet, probiotics, or even fecal transplants may improve mental health symptoms.

So, what does all this mean for loneliness and social behavior? Firstly, it suggests that our social behavior may be influenced, in part, by our gut microbiota. If loneliness can alter our gut microbiota, and our gut can, in turn, affect our brain and behavior, this creates a potential feedback loop. We may feel lonely, which could affect our gut, which then impacts our brain, potentially increasing feelings of social withdrawal or anxiety. However, more research is needed to fully understand these interactions.

Secondly, this research opens up exciting potential interventions for loneliness. If our gut microbiota can influence our social behavior, then modifying our gut microbiota may be a way to influence feelings of loneliness. This could involve dietary changes, like increasing fiber intake to promote a healthy gut microbiome, or potentially using probiotics.

It's crucial, however, not to oversimplify these relationships or potential interventions. The gut-brain axis is complex and influenced by numerous factors, including genetics, diet, stress, and more. Plus, our understanding of it is still in its infancy, especially regarding its role in complex behaviors like social interaction. However, with continued research, we may, in the future, have a whole new set of tools to combat loneliness, from our diet to tailored probiotics.

While we wait for this research to evolve, it's worth noting that a balanced, diverse diet is known to be beneficial for gut health, which is likely to be beneficial for overall health, including mental health. Engaging in stress reduction activities like meditation, maintaining a regular sleep pattern, and regular exercise are all strategies known to promote both gut and mental health.

The burgeoning research on the gut-brain axis and its potential impact on social behavior is an exciting new frontier in our understanding of loneliness. As this field of study progresses, we may be able to offer increasingly nuanced advice to those struggling with feelings of social isolation, moving beyond the current prescriptions to engage in more social activities or seek psychological support. The potential for treatments based on diet or probiotics to influence the gut-brain axis and, consequently, feelings of loneliness, is an encouraging prospect.

We must also remain mindful that while the potential of gut-brain axis research is immense, it does not mean that loneliness is entirely a product of our biology. It's an emotion affected by a complex interaction of many factors, including our social environment, personal psychology, economic conditions, and indeed, possibly, our gut microbiome. We also must acknowledge that while we wait for the science to progress, people are suffering from loneliness now, and we need immediate, practical, and accessible solutions.

Although the journey to uncover the complex interplay of our gut and brain and its influence on our social behaviors has just begun, it is a journey that holds promise. The more we understand about the human body and its interconnected systems, the better we will be at addressing and potentially alleviating the loneliness epidemic.

The gut-brain axis research underscores the importance of a holistic approach to mental health. Our minds are not isolated from our bodies, and our social health isn't disconnected from our physical health. As we continue to delve deeper into this field of study, we may discover more about how every aspect of our lives, from the food we eat to the company we keep, can have profound effects on our mental well-being.

As researchers continue to unravel the intricate communication systems within our bodies, the mysteries of loneliness will hopefully become more manageable. The loneliness epidemic, like many of our modern health crises, needs an interdisciplinary approach, embracing new frontiers like the gut-brain axis, to find comprehensive solutions. In this journey, we need to remember that every step forward, even if it is a small one, helps us get closer to our goal of understanding and overcoming the crisis of social isolation.

Physiological Changes Caused by Loneliness and Strategies for Mitigation

As we dive deeper into the effects of loneliness, it becomes evident that it isn't just a mental health issue. Loneliness can cause profound physiological changes within our bodies, leading to severe health problems. Understanding these effects can help us develop strategies to mitigate them, offering those suffering from loneliness much-needed relief.

Loneliness activates a series of processes in the body that are part of our stress response. This stress response is beneficial in short-term situations where we need to fight or flee. However, when loneliness becomes chronic, this constant activation of the stress response can lead to numerous health problems.

The body responds to loneliness in the same way it would a physical threat. The autonomic nervous system gets involved, triggering a cascade of hormones that leads to an increase in heart rate, blood pressure, and levels of the stress hormone cortisol. While cortisol helps prepare the body to respond to acute stressors, its chronic elevation is associated with numerous health problems such as obesity, diabetes, heart diseases, and a weakened immune system.

In addition to the effects on our hormonal system, loneliness can also lead to inflammation. Research shows that socially isolated individuals have higher levels of inflammatory markers in their blood. Inflammation is a critical component of our immune system's response to injury or infection, but when it becomes chronic, it can damage healthy tissues and organs, leading to diseases like cancer, heart disease, and Alzheimer's.

Now that we've established the physiological changes loneliness can bring, what are some strategies to mitigate these effects?

Physical Activity

Regular physical activity is one of the most effective ways to combat the physiological effects of loneliness. Exercise reduces cortisol levels, lowers blood pressure, and improves immune function. Additionally, physical activity increases the production of endorphins, chemicals in the brain that act as natural painkillers and mood elevators. This can help to counter some of the negative emotional effects of loneliness.

Healthy Eating

A balanced diet, rich in fruits, vegetables, lean proteins, and whole grains, can help counteract inflammation caused by loneliness. Certain foods, such as those rich in omega-3 fatty acids (e.g., fatty fish, walnuts) and antioxidants (e.g., berries, dark chocolate), have been shown to reduce inflammation.

Mindfulness and Relaxation Techniques

Practices such as mindfulness, meditation, and yoga can help reduce cortisol levels and lower blood pressure. These practices can also help individuals become more aware of their feelings of loneliness and provide them with tools to manage these feelings more effectively.

Social Interaction

While it may seem obvious, it's worth reiterating that increasing social interactions is a vital strategy in combating loneliness. This doesn't mean you have to be surrounded by people all the time. Quality of connections matters more than quantity. Meaningful interactions, even if infrequent, can help to reduce feelings of loneliness.

Psychotherapy

Therapy, particularly cognitive-behavioral therapy (CBT), can help individuals understand and change thought patterns leading to feelings of loneliness. Through CBT, individuals can learn strategies to manage feelings of loneliness, improve their social skills, and boost their self-esteem.

Community Engagement

Engaging in community activities, such as volunteer work, can provide a sense of purpose and belonging, alleviating feelings of loneliness. Community engagement not only offers opportunities for social interaction but also can give individuals a sense of being part of something bigger than themselves, which can be very fulfilling.

Loneliness doesn't just affect our minds but can also lead to serious physiological changes. However, by understanding these changes, we can develop strategies to mitigate these effects. Whether it's through physical activity, healthy eating, mindfulness practices, therapy, or community engagement, there are many ways to combat these physiological changes.

Digital Detox

In our modern world, where digital connections often replace face-to-face interactions, a "digital detox" can be surprisingly beneficial. Setting aside time to disconnect from digital devices and engage in real-world activities can reduce feelings of loneliness. This step can also lower the risk of developing "technostress," a condition resulting from excessive use of digital technology.

Health Check-ups

Regular health check-ups can help monitor the physiological changes related to loneliness. They can also help catch any resulting health problems early on. For instance, consistent high blood pressure readings may be a sign of chronic loneliness. Regular monitoring can help you and your healthcare provider take necessary steps to mitigate the effects of loneliness on your physical health.

Nature Therapy

Spending time in nature, also known as forest bathing or nature therapy, can have significant benefits in reducing feelings of loneliness and its physiological effects. The calming effect of nature on our minds helps to decrease stress hormone levels, lowers blood pressure, and enhances the immune system. This practice has been particularly beneficial for urban dwellers who experience high levels of isolation.

Pets

Having a pet, especially a dog or a cat, can provide companionship that can alleviate feelings of loneliness. Pets offer unconditional love and affection, increasing levels of oxytocin, the so-called "love hormone," which can combat stress and lower cortisol levels.

Support Groups

Joining support groups, where people with similar experiences come together, can also help. Sharing experiences with others who are going through the same situation makes one feel less alone and more understood. It also provides a sense of community that can lessen feelings of loneliness.

Ultimately, the key to mitigating the physiological changes caused by loneliness lies in addressing the root cause - our human need for meaningful social connection.

By maintaining healthy lifestyle habits, practicing mindfulness, seeking therapy, engaging in community activities, and using tools like support groups, we can not only alleviate feelings of loneliness but also its physiological effects.

Remember, it's perfectly okay to seek help, and reaching out to others is the first significant step in overcoming loneliness.

Chapter 6: Loneliness Across the Lifespan

Childhood and Adolescent Loneliness: Unique Challenges and Solutions

Loneliness is not a condition limited to adulthood or old age. It reaches out its insidious tendrils into all age brackets, including children and adolescents. This chapter aims to shed light on the unique challenges and the consequent solutions that are pertinent to tackling loneliness in these younger populations.

Firstly, it's important to clarify that solitude doesn't automatically translate to loneliness for children and adolescents. Young individuals, much like adults, require a healthy balance of social interaction and solitude for overall development. It is when this solitude becomes chronic, and there is an absence of quality social connections that loneliness sets in, leading to various negative impacts on mental and physical health.

Unique Challenges of Childhood and Adolescent Loneliness

The first significant challenge is the identification of loneliness. Young children, in particular, might lack the necessary vocabulary to articulate their feelings of loneliness. Adolescents, on the other hand, might feel apprehensive about voicing their loneliness due to the stigma associated with it.

Another challenge lies in the impact of social media and technology. While these platforms promise connection, they can often result in feelings of exclusion and can intensify feelings of loneliness. The impact of cyberbullying is also a notable concern in this regard.

There is a strong link between loneliness in young people and mental health issues such as anxiety and depression. Adolescent loneliness, in particular, is associated with an increased risk of depression and suicidal ideation.

Furthermore, childhood and adolescent loneliness can lead to social withdrawal, fostering a vicious cycle that deepens the sense of isolation.

Strategies for Mitigation

Addressing these unique challenges requires a multifaceted approach.

Open Communication and Active Listening

The first step in combating loneliness in children and adolescents is fostering open communication. Parents, caregivers, teachers, and other significant adults in a child's life should encourage children to express their feelings and thoughts. This open dialogue can help identify feelings of loneliness early on.

Fostering Quality Relationships

The quality of relationships is more important than quantity. Encourage children and teenagers to build deeper connections with their peers, family members, and other significant figures in their lives. Quality connections can provide the emotional support and validation needed to combat feelings of loneliness.

Teaching Social Skills

Children and adolescents need to be taught essential social skills like empathy, conflict resolution, assertiveness, and emotional regulation. These skills can help them establish and maintain healthy relationships.

Safe Use of Technology

Educating young individuals about the safe and healthy use of technology is crucial. While technology can be a double-edged sword, if used correctly, it can serve as a tool for connection rather than a source of isolation.

Professional Help

If feelings of loneliness persist, it might be beneficial to seek professional help. Mental health professionals can provide the necessary guidance and therapy to help children and teenagers navigate their feelings of loneliness.

Addressing loneliness in childhood and adolescence requires recognizing the unique challenges they face and adopting tailored strategies for intervention. By fostering open communication, teaching social skills, ensuring the safe use of technology, and encouraging quality relationships, we can help them navigate the tumultuous waters of loneliness, paving the way for healthier, happier adults.

Loneliness in Adults: Navigating Social Isolation in the Prime of Life

Adult life is often equated with independence, stability, and the establishment of significant relationships. However, it also represents a phase where social networks might shrink due to life changes, and loneliness can sneak in, often unnoticed until it starts taking a toll. Understanding this crucial stage of life can help us recognize the specific challenges that adults face and offer meaningful solutions.

Unique Challenges of Adult Loneliness

Adults face a unique set of circumstances that can lead to loneliness. A significant life change, such as relocation for work, can lead to isolation, as establishing new social connections might be challenging. The breakup of a significant relationship or the loss of a loved one can lead to devastating loneliness. Additionally, the transition to parenthood often comes with a drastic shift in social dynamics, which can lead to feelings of isolation.

At the same time, adults are expected to be more resilient and resourceful in coping with such life changes, making it more challenging to ask for help when loneliness hits.

Another contributing factor to loneliness in adults is the societal pressure to achieve specific milestones like a stable career, marriage, or parenthood. Falling behind these socially prescribed timelines can lead to feelings of exclusion and loneliness.

Strategies for Mitigation

Addressing loneliness in adults requires interventions tailored to their specific needs and circumstances.

Developing Meaningful Relationships

As adults, there can be a tendency to focus on roles, responsibilities, and achievements at the cost of relationships. However, nurturing existing relationships and fostering new ones can provide a buffer against loneliness. Joining community groups, volunteering, or engaging in activities of interest can lead to meaningful connections.

Embracing Life Transitions

Major life transitions, whether it be moving to a new city, changing careers, or becoming a parent, often bring about a sense of loneliness. It's important to accept that these feelings are normal. Seeking support during these times, either through friends, family, or professional counselors, can help navigate these transitions smoothly.

Practicing Self-Care

Self-care plays a crucial role in managing loneliness. This can involve regular exercise, maintaining a balanced diet, and ensuring adequate sleep. Engaging in activities that provide joy and relaxation, like reading, hiking, or meditation, can also foster a positive mindset.

Seeking Professional Help

If feelings of loneliness persist or lead to symptoms of depression, anxiety, or other mental health conditions, seeking help from a mental health professional is essential. Therapies like cognitive-behavioral therapy (CBT) can help manage negative thought patterns related to loneliness.

Embracing Technology

While it's true that excessive technology use can lead to feelings of isolation, when used thoughtfully, it can be a tool for connection. Video calls, online forums, and social media can bridge the gap of physical distance and allow for the maintenance of existing relationships and the formation of new ones.

Mindfulness and Acceptance

It's crucial to accept that it's okay to feel lonely. Recognizing and acknowledging these feelings without self-judgment is the first step towards addressing them. Techniques like mindfulness can help stay grounded in the present moment and reduce feelings of loneliness.

In conclusion, while adults face a unique set of challenges when it comes to loneliness, with understanding, intervention, and support, they can successfully navigate these challenges. Ultimately, overcoming loneliness involves the collective effort of individuals, communities, and society at large.

The Plight of the Elderly: Coping with Loneliness in the Golden Years

Ageing is often marked with a plethora of life changes: retirement, health decline, and loss of loved ones, to name a few. These changes may lead to social isolation and loneliness, particularly acute in the elderly. Let's delve into the unique challenges the elderly population faces and propose targeted strategies to alleviate loneliness.

Challenges Faced by the Elderly

Loneliness in the elderly can stem from multiple factors. It often coincides with other significant life changes, such as retirement, health issues, or the loss of a spouse or close friends. Retirement can lead to a loss of daily structure, work identity, and social interaction, contributing to feelings of loneliness. Moreover, health issues can lead to reduced mobility, making it harder to engage in social activities.

Furthermore, the experience of grief and bereavement can be isolating. Losing a life partner can especially lead to profound loneliness. Additionally, outliving many of their peers can make the elderly feel alone and disconnected.

A critical aspect is the societal attitudes towards ageing. The societal emphasis on youthfulness and productivity can make the elderly feel neglected and undervalued, exacerbating feelings of loneliness.

Strategies for Mitigation

While these challenges may seem daunting, there are ways to manage and even alleviate loneliness in the elderly. Here are some strategies.

Promote Active Aging

Active aging includes regular physical activity, social engagement, and cognitive stimulation. Physical activity, such as light walking or chair exercises, can improve health and well-being. Social activities could include joining clubs, volunteering, or participating in community events. Activities that stimulate the mind, such as puzzles or reading, can keep the mind sharp and engaged.

Facilitate Meaningful Connections

Fostering connections with family, friends, and the community can have a tremendous impact on reducing loneliness. Regular visits, phone calls, or letters can provide a sense of belonging. Encourage the elderly to engage in social activities, such as joining senior centers or community groups. These spaces can provide a platform for shared experiences and friendships.

Encourage Life Review and Legacy Activities

Legacy activities, such as writing memoirs or recording family histories, can provide a sense of purpose and continuity. This process allows the elderly to reflect on their lives, process experiences, and pass on wisdom to younger generations. It can provide a sense of accomplishment and connection, reducing feelings of loneliness.

Enhance Accessibility and Mobility

Limited mobility can significantly restrict social activities, contributing to loneliness. Therefore, ensuring a safe and accessible living environment is critical. This could involve mobility aids, transportation services, or home modifications to facilitate independence and social interaction.

Utilize Technology

Technology can be a powerful tool in mitigating loneliness. Video calls can bridge the gap between loved ones who live far away. Online platforms can connect the elderly with others who share similar interests. However, it's important to provide the necessary support and education for the elderly to comfortably use these technologies.

Seek Professional Help

If feelings of loneliness persist or contribute to mental health issues, professional help may be required. This could involve therapy or counseling services that specialize in geriatric mental health. Home care services can also provide companionship and support.

Promote Intergenerational Relationships

Promoting relationships between the elderly and younger generations can provide mutual benefits. The elderly can share wisdom and experiences, while younger individuals can provide companionship and tech assistance. Intergenerational programs can foster understanding, respect, and reduce feelings of loneliness.

While ageing comes with its own set of challenges, loneliness doesn't have to be an inevitable part of the golden years. With the right strategies, support, and societal attitudes, the elderly can enjoy a connected, fulfilling life.

While many initiatives can help alleviate loneliness in the elderly, it's essential to continue to discuss and enhance them.

Improve Social Infrastructure

Our social infrastructure, such as parks, libraries, and community centers, plays a critical role in fostering interaction and connectivity. Improving the accessibility and senior-friendliness of these public spaces can significantly encourage the elderly to venture out and interact with their communities. In designing these spaces, we should aim for barrier-free and safe environments that cater to the physical limitations that may come with age.

Promote Age-Friendly Communities

Age-friendly communities are designed to promote active ageing by optimizing opportunities for health, participation, and security. Such communities adapt their structures and services to be accessible and inclusive to older people with varying needs and capacities. The promotion of age-friendly communities goes beyond infrastructure—it includes supportive social and health services, opportunities for civic participation, and initiatives that promote inclusion and challenge ageism.

Encourage Lifelong Learning

Lifelong learning initiatives can significantly contribute to reducing feelings of loneliness and isolation. By encouraging the elderly to learn new skills, we not only engage them cognitively but also provide opportunities for social interaction. Consider book clubs, art classes, or even digital literacy courses. Learning new skills can boost confidence and foster a sense of achievement, which can be crucial for maintaining mental health in later life.

Create Volunteer Opportunities

Many elderly people have a wealth of experience and wisdom to share. Volunteering gives them an opportunity to remain active, both physically and mentally. It allows them to feel valued by contributing to their communities and promotes a sense of purpose and belonging. Some might find fulfillment in mentoring younger generations, while others may prefer roles related to their previous work skills or hobbies.

Support Caregivers

Last but certainly not least, supporting caregivers is an essential part of the puzzle. Caregiving can be an emotionally taxing role, potentially leading to burnout and feelings of isolation. By providing respite care, education, and support groups, we can help ensure caregivers maintain their well-being, which in turn allows them to better support the elderly individuals in their care.

In short, mitigating loneliness in the elderly is not an insurmountable task—it just requires thoughtful attention, comprehensive strategies, and ongoing dedication.

By considering these strategies, we can ensure that the golden years truly are a time of fulfillment and connection, minimizing the specter of loneliness that all too often casts a shadow on this, what should be, a thoroughly enjoyable stage of life.

Chapter 7: The Impact of Pandemics on Loneliness

Case Study: COVID-19 and Its Amplification of Loneliness

In the annals of human history, pandemics have left indelible marks on societies and individuals. The recent COVID-19 pandemic is no exception. To curb the spread of the virus, countries worldwide implemented various measures, including travel restrictions, lockdowns, and social distancing. While necessary for public health, these measures inadvertently created another crisis: a crisis of loneliness.

The nature of the COVID-19 pandemic amplified loneliness in several ways, impacting different sections of society and exacerbating existing inequalities.

Increased Social Isolation

Social distancing measures have led to an unavoidable increase in social isolation. Regular social interactions, such as catching up with friends, attending communal events, or merely engaging in casual banter with colleagues at the office, were abruptly curtailed. As humans, we are wired for connection and social interaction, and when it's suddenly taken away, we experience profound feelings of loneliness.

Technology: A Double-Edged Sword

The use of technology skyrocketed during the pandemic as people sought to connect in new ways. Virtual meetings, online classes, and digital gatherings became the new norm. However, this shift was a double-edged sword. While technology allowed us to maintain some level of social interaction, it also highlighted the digital divide. Many, especially the elderly or those from lower socioeconomic backgrounds, lacked access to technology or the necessary skills to use it, leaving them even more isolated.

Mental Health Crisis

COVID-19 induced a significant amount of stress and anxiety, contributing to the loneliness crisis. Concerns about contracting the virus, uncertainty about the future, and the economic impact of the pandemic weighed heavily on people's minds. This added psychological burden exacerbated feelings of isolation.

A Sense of Loss

The pandemic also brought a profound sense of loss. Many people lost loved ones to the virus, while others experienced the loss of normalcy, routine, and security. Grieving in isolation, without the typical rituals or the physical presence of supportive friends and family, intensified feelings of loneliness.

Solutions and Resilience

Faced with the complex challenge of managing a global pandemic and a growing epidemic of loneliness, societies had to get creative. Various initiatives emerged aimed at mitigating the impact of COVID-19 on social isolation. These ranged from mental health hotlines to virtual support groups and community outreach programs for the elderly.

One of the most inspiring outcomes of the pandemic was the demonstration of community resilience. People stepped up to support each other, forming local support groups, checking in on neighbors, and volunteering in different capacities. This increased community cohesion has the potential to outlast the pandemic itself and could be harnessed to combat loneliness in the long term.

As we move forward, the lessons learned from COVID-19 will be invaluable in managing the loneliness epidemic. It's clear that crises like these can amplify existing social issues, including loneliness. However, they can also highlight areas for improvement and provide an impetus for developing more resilient, connected, and supportive communities.

We are now more aware than ever of the importance of social connectivity for our mental well-being. As we navigate the post-pandemic world, let's keep this awareness front and center, informing our policies, programs, and personal behaviors, so we can better prevent and mitigate loneliness, both in times of crisis and in periods of stability. The pandemic may have amplified the crisis of loneliness, but it also gives us an opportunity to respond in ways that strengthen our social fabric, allowing us to emerge stronger, more resilient, and more connected than before.

Mental Health in a Post-Pandemic World

As we find ourselves in the throes of a post-pandemic world, it is critical to take stock of the profound and wide-ranging effects the pandemic has had on our mental health. From heightened feelings of anxiety and stress to amplified loneliness and depression, the mental health consequences of the COVID-19 pandemic are far-reaching and complex.

The Pandemic's Effect on Mental Health

The pandemic created a perfect storm for mental health issues to thrive. Uncertainty about the virus, the fear of infection, and the grief over the loss of loved ones have induced widespread psychological stress. Moreover, economic instability, unemployment, and disruption of routine life patterns have contributed to the feeling of being out of control and fueled anxiety and depression. This perfect storm was further aggravated by the physical isolation measures, which led to an increase in loneliness and its associated mental health risks.

Post-Pandemic Mental Health Landscape

As we emerge from the pandemic, the psychological repercussions of this global crisis will likely continue to reverberate. We must be prepared for a possible surge in mental health disorders and prioritize psychological well-being as a critical aspect of recovery.

However, the post-pandemic mental health landscape isn't necessarily all doom and gloom. The collective experience of the pandemic has shone a spotlight on mental health like never before. It has brought the conversation about mental health to the forefront, driving increased awareness, understanding, and a decreased stigma around mental health issues. These changes could potentially lead to better mental health policies, practices, and support systems in the future.

Navigating Mental Health in a Post-Pandemic World

The key to navigating mental health in a post-pandemic world lies in acknowledging and addressing the psychological repercussions of the pandemic and implementing strategies for prevention, early detection, and treatment of mental health disorders. Here are a few strategies:

- **Community-Based Support:** The role of community-based support systems in combating loneliness and promoting mental health cannot be overemphasized. Community groups can provide a sense of belonging, reduce feelings of isolation, and offer emotional support. They can also facilitate early identification of mental health issues and act as a bridge to professional help.

- **Professional Mental Health Services:** Access to quality professional mental health services is crucial. Efforts should be made to improve the availability and affordability of these services. This includes removing barriers to access, such as reducing waiting times, expanding teletherapy options, and ensuring mental health coverage in health insurance plans.
- **Workplace Mental Health Programs:** Employers can play a significant role in supporting the mental health of their employees. This can be achieved through the implementation of workplace mental health programs, which might include providing access to mental health resources, promoting work-life balance, and cultivating a supportive work environment.
- **Mindfulness and Self-Care:** Mindfulness practices, such as meditation and yoga, have been shown to reduce stress, anxiety, and depression. Incorporating these practices into daily routines can help individuals cope with the psychological impacts of the pandemic.

The Future of Mental Health

While the post-pandemic world poses significant mental health challenges, it also offers an opportunity to reshape the mental health landscape. The widespread psychological impacts of the pandemic have underscored the necessity of integrating mental health into all aspects of health and social policy. It's become clear that mental health is not just about treating mental illnesses. It's about promoting mental well-being, preventing mental disorders, and enabling recovery from these disorders.

The post-pandemic world presents an opportunity for individuals, communities, and societies to rally together and create more supportive, resilient, and mentally healthy societies. The task might be daunting, but the potential benefits — a world where mental health is recognized, prioritized, and cared for — are enormous and well worth the effort.

In our collective journey towards improved mental health in the post-pandemic world, we must remember that change begins at the individual level. Every step we take to manage our own mental health effectively and extend compassion and support to others around us contributes to this broader goal.

Harnessing Digital Tools

One of the ways in which the pandemic has reshaped our world is the increased reliance on technology for work, education, communication, and entertainment. This digital transformation has significant implications for mental health, both positive and negative. On the positive side, digital tools, including mental health apps, online therapy platforms, and virtual support groups, have become increasingly important in providing mental health support during periods of isolation and lockdown. These tools can continue to play a vital role in the post-pandemic world, offering accessible, flexible, and cost-effective mental health solutions.

However, it's crucial to be aware of the potential drawbacks of this digital reliance. Excessive screen time, online harassment, and the stress of constant connectivity can all have detrimental effects on mental health. It's important to find balance and set boundaries when using digital tools. For example, you might designate certain times of day as "technology-free" to disconnect and recharge.

Role of Physical Activity and Nature

The mental health benefits of physical activity and spending time in nature are well-established. Regular exercise can reduce anxiety and depression, improve mood, and enhance self-esteem. Similarly, exposure to nature has been shown to reduce stress, increase relaxation, and improve mood and cognitive functioning. In the post-pandemic world, incorporating physical activity and time in nature into daily routines can be a powerful strategy for promoting mental health and combating loneliness.

Investing in Mental Health Research

Finally, investment in mental health research is crucial. The pandemic has posed unprecedented challenges and raised many unanswered questions about mental health. Continued research is needed to understand the full impact of the pandemic on mental health, identify at-risk groups, and develop effective interventions. This research can help us not only navigate the post-pandemic world but also prepare for future public health crises.

Navigating mental health in a post-pandemic world requires collective efforts at the individual, community, and societal levels. It involves acknowledging and addressing the psychological impacts of the pandemic, fostering supportive and resilient communities, harnessing the power of digital tools, promoting physical activity and nature exposure, and investing in mental health research. With these strategies, we can work towards a future where mental health is valued, prioritized, and cared for — a future where no one has to face the challenges of loneliness and mental health disorders alone.

Lessons Learned and Preparing for Future Global Crises

The crisis of loneliness has been simmering below the surface of global consciousness for many years. However, the COVID-19 pandemic, with its widespread social isolation and drastic changes to everyday life, has brought this issue to the forefront. As we navigate the recovery process, we need to extract valuable lessons from our experiences and prepare ourselves for any future global crises.

Lesson 1: The Interconnectedness of Our World

One of the most significant lessons the pandemic has taught us is how interconnected our world truly is. Viruses and emotions alike do not respect geographical boundaries; they spread and influence people globally. This interconnectedness means that a problem occurring in one part of the world can quickly become an issue for everyone.

Similarly, the phenomenon of loneliness is not confined to any one community or country. It is a universal experience, and its solutions must also be global in nature. This global mindset involves sharing resources and information, collaborating on research, and implementing strategies that recognize the shared nature of our experiences.

Lesson 2: The Importance of Mental Health

The pandemic has underscored the critical importance of mental health. As physical health took center stage, the parallel epidemic of loneliness and mental health disorders emerged from the shadows. Suddenly, the entire world was compelled to acknowledge these issues.

Moving forward, it's imperative that mental health retains its newfound priority status. Investment in mental health research and resources, destigmatization efforts, and improved access to mental health care are all necessary steps.

Lesson 3: Community Matters

The experience of widespread isolation and loneliness underscored the fundamental human need for community. The value of relationships, human connection, and mutual support became starkly evident in their absence.

In future, communities should be prepared to respond swiftly and efficiently to ensure that social connection is maintained in crisis situations. This preparation might involve creating plans for virtual socialization or support networks, or developing community resources to reach vulnerable individuals.

Lesson 4: Resilience and Adaptation

The pandemic also highlighted human capacity for resilience and adaptation. Despite the profound challenges, individuals, communities, and societies found ways to adapt and navigate the crisis.

This resilience is a beacon of hope for future crises. We have learned that change, even drastic, unexpected change, is something we can manage. However, it's vital to remember that resilience is not just a personal trait; it's nurtured by supportive environments and resources. So, fostering resilience must be a collective effort.

Preparing for Future Crises
Invest in Mental Health Infrastructure

Preparing for future crises begins with robust investment in mental health infrastructure. This includes funding mental health services, research, and public education initiatives. Strengthening this infrastructure will ensure that when the next crisis hits, mental health resources are readily available to those in need.

Build Strong, Resilient Communities

As we've learned, community support is a powerful tool in combating loneliness and promoting mental health. Efforts should be made to foster strong, interconnected communities that can provide support in times of crisis. This involves building social networks, providing community resources, and promoting a culture of mutual support and care.

Develop Emergency Response Plans

Emergency response plans shouldn't be limited to physical health crises. They should also include strategies for maintaining mental health and social connection in crisis situations. These plans might involve deploying mental health professionals, setting up virtual support networks, or providing resources for at-home mental health care.

Promote Healthy Lifestyle Habits

Encouraging healthy lifestyle habits is another critical preventative measure. Regular physical activity, balanced nutrition, adequate sleep, and mindfulness practices can all boost mental health and resilience. By promoting these habits now, we can equip individuals with the tools to manage stress and anxiety in crisis situations of the future.

Integrate Technology Mindfully

The pandemic has pushed us towards a greater reliance on technology for connection. However, as we've seen, digital communication cannot fully replace face-to-face interaction. While online communication has its place, it should be seen as a complement rather than a replacement for in-person connections. Hence, moving forward, it will be essential to understand how we can use technology effectively and mindfully.

Developing platforms that facilitate real, meaningful connections will be key. More importantly, creating guidelines around the usage of such technology is vital so it supports mental health rather than hindering it. This may involve setting boundaries around screen time, using technology-free zones and times, and integrating online interactions with offline ones.

Prioritize Research and Understanding

Despite the lessons learned so far, there is still much we don't understand about loneliness, mental health, and how to combat these issues effectively. More research is required, not only to understand the factors driving these conditions but also to test interventions and their effectiveness in diverse populations and contexts.

As part of this, it's important to examine the effects of major global crises on loneliness and mental health and derive further lessons from these experiences. Research initiatives should be adequately funded, and findings must be disseminated to the public and policy-makers to inform future decision-making.

Create Policies that Support Mental Health

Lastly, we need policies that reflect the importance of mental health. This involves both healthcare policies and broader societal policies, including those related to work, education, and community development. Such policies should consider mental health as a key component of overall health and wellbeing, rather than an afterthought.

Examples might include mandating mental health education in schools, implementing mental health-friendly workplace policies (such as flexible working hours, work-from-home options, and mental health days), and investing in community resources that facilitate social connection.

The pandemic has shown us that loneliness and mental health issues are critical global challenges that we can't afford to ignore. As we rebuild and prepare for future crises, these lessons must inform our actions. Only by placing mental health and human connection at the forefront of our efforts can we hope to prevent another epidemic of loneliness and create a more resilient, connected society.

Public Health Response to Social Isolation in Pandemics

Throughout our journey in this book, we've discussed the interconnections of loneliness and social isolation with various other aspects of life and health, particularly in the context of pandemics. This chapter aims to specifically delve into the public health response to this critical issue, identifying potential solutions and ways to enhance our resilience against the backdrop of future crises.

Recognizing Loneliness as a Public Health Issue

The first step is the recognition of loneliness as a public health issue. Historically, loneliness has been viewed as a private, personal issue, but the evidence clearly shows that it has widespread implications for health and well-being. Therefore, integrating the management of loneliness and social isolation into public health planning is crucial. This recognition will help justify the allocation of resources to study and combat these problems.

Implementing Health Communication Strategies

During a pandemic or any other public health crisis, transparent, regular, and accurate communication is essential. This includes providing clear guidelines about protective measures, informing the public about the progression of the pandemic, and offering guidance on managing social isolation and loneliness. Public health authorities should leverage various mediums, including social media, traditional media, and text message services, to reach different demographics.

Beyond the pandemic-specific communication, there's also a need for mental health education and stigma reduction campaigns. These could include information on recognizing signs of loneliness and mental health problems, tips for self-care, and resources for getting help.

Enhancing Access to Mental Health Services

Increasing the availability and accessibility of mental health services is paramount during a pandemic. This can be achieved in several ways. One approach is through telehealth, which involves delivering health services, including mental health care, through digital platforms. Telehealth not only reduces the risk of virus transmission but also breaks down geographical barriers, making care accessible for those living in remote areas.

Yet, while telehealth can be a valuable tool, it's important to acknowledge that it's not suitable or accessible for everyone. Therefore, efforts should also be made to ensure the availability of in-person services wherever it is safe and feasible to do so.

Promoting Community Resilience

At the heart of a robust public health response to social isolation in pandemics is the promotion of community resilience. Encouraging neighborliness, kindness, and social responsibility can help to mitigate feelings of loneliness and build a sense of community, even in the context of physical distancing.

Public health authorities can facilitate this through various initiatives. For instance, they could support community-led projects that aim to connect people virtually or in a safe, physically distanced manner. They could also promote volunteering opportunities, which have been shown to enhance feelings of social connectedness and purpose.

Investing in Research and Surveillance

Finally, continued investment in research and surveillance is crucial to guide public health responses. Data on the prevalence and impacts of social isolation and loneliness should be routinely collected and analyzed, and research should be conducted to identify the most effective interventions for different populations.

While pandemics undoubtedly pose significant challenges to social connectivity and mental health, they also provide opportunities to reconsider our public health approaches.

By recognizing loneliness as a public health issue, implementing effective communication strategies, enhancing access to mental health services, promoting community resilience, and investing in research, we can build a society that is not only resilient in the face of future pandemics but also healthier and more connected overall.

Chapter 8: Counteracting the Loneliness Epidemic: Existing Strategies

Policies and Initiatives to Combat Loneliness: An International Perspective

As we've highlighted, loneliness is a global issue with significant implications for public health. However, various countries have adopted different strategies to tackle this issue. This chapter offers a comparative perspective on these strategies and the lessons that can be learned from them.

United Kingdom: A Minister for Loneliness

In a historic move, the UK government appointed its first 'Minister for Loneliness' in 2018. The role was created in response to a report highlighting loneliness as a significant public health issue, likening its impact to that of smoking 15 cigarettes a day.

The UK has implemented various strategies to address loneliness, including the development of a national strategy that sets out a comprehensive vision for tackling loneliness in England. It features a myriad of proposed actions, including the provision of social prescribing by healthcare professionals. Social prescribing involves referring patients experiencing loneliness to local, non-clinical services like community activities and volunteering.

Australia: Friends for Good

Australia, grappling with its loneliness epidemic, has seen the emergence of organizations like 'Friends for Good,' a not-for-profit entity with the mission of raising awareness about loneliness, its causes, and its impact on health. One of its most innovative initiatives is 'FriendLine,' a national telephone service that people can call when they're feeling lonely.

Japan: Creating Connection Through Social Activities

In Japan, where the loneliness epidemic is particularly pronounced among the elderly, different strategies have been adopted. One such strategy is the creation of 'community salons,' local hubs where elderly residents can participate in activities like arts and crafts or exercise classes. These salons are aimed at providing opportunities for social interaction and alleviating feelings of isolation and loneliness.

Canada: Advancing Mental Health Services

Canada, recognizing the connection between loneliness and mental health, has advanced its mental health services to include a focus on social isolation. The Mental Health

Commission of Canada (MHCC) provides a number of resources, including a toolkit for organizations to assess and address social isolation.

Lessons Learned and Looking Ahead

While each country has its unique approach to combating loneliness, several common themes emerge. Firstly, the importance of recognizing and validating loneliness as a public health issue is crucial. Secondly, a multi-faceted approach that includes policy initiatives, community programs, and healthcare system changes is necessary.

Lastly, addressing loneliness requires a community-wide effort. From the public sector to not-for-profit organizations, healthcare professionals, community groups, and even individuals, everyone has a part to play in tackling the loneliness epidemic.

As we look towards the future, the task at hand is to continue learning from each other's experiences and to refine our strategies in addressing loneliness. It's a collective effort that requires understanding, empathy, innovation, and most importantly, a shared sense of responsibility. By building on the initiatives discussed here and continuing to innovate, we can make headway in addressing the loneliness epidemic.

Promoting Mental Health Awareness and Support

Tackling loneliness also requires addressing the mental health issues it often accompanies, such as depression and anxiety. Promoting mental health awareness and support are essential steps in this process.

Understanding the Connection

Mental health awareness begins with understanding that loneliness and mental health issues are closely intertwined. The feelings of isolation can lead to conditions like depression and anxiety, while these conditions can also exacerbate feelings of loneliness. This is a vicious cycle that we need to break.

But why is loneliness connected to mental health issues? It's believed that our brains interpret loneliness as a threat, triggering a stress response. Over time, this stress response can lead to various mental and physical health problems. Understanding this connection can help us see why promoting mental health awareness and support is a crucial component of tackling loneliness.

Promoting Awareness

Promoting awareness about mental health involves reducing stigma, encouraging conversations, and educating the public. Social media platforms, community events, workplace initiatives, and education systems can all be effective venues for spreading mental health awareness.

1. **Reducing Stigma**: One of the biggest barriers to mental health support is the stigma associated with mental health issues. Campaigns like the UK's 'Time to Change' initiative have been effective in encouraging people to talk openly about mental health, helping to reduce stigma.
2. **Encouraging Conversations**: Encouraging conversations about mental health can help people understand that they're not alone and that support is available. This can be achieved through community forums, social media, and even in workplaces.
3. **Education**: Schools, colleges, and universities have a critical role to play in promoting mental health awareness. By incorporating mental health education into their curriculum, these institutions can equip young people with the knowledge they need to understand and manage their mental health.

Offering Support

Once awareness has been raised, it's crucial to provide avenues for support. Support can come in various forms, including professional help, community support groups, online resources, and self-care practices.

1. **Professional Help**: Mental health professionals, including psychologists, psychiatrists, and counsellors, play a vital role in providing support. They can offer therapies and treatments tailored to an individual's needs.

2. **Community Support Groups**: These groups can offer a sense of community and understanding that individuals might not get elsewhere. The shared experiences can provide comfort, reduce feelings of isolation, and promote healing.

3. **Online Resources**: The internet is a valuable tool for providing mental health support. Websites and apps can provide resources, self-help tools, and even therapy options that individuals can access from the comfort of their homes.

4. **Self-Care Practices**: Encouraging self-care practices is another important aspect of mental health support. This might involve promoting physical activity, healthy eating, mindfulness, or relaxation techniques.

Promoting mental health awareness and support is an essential part of tackling the loneliness epidemic. It involves understanding the connection between loneliness and mental health, raising awareness about mental health issues, and providing robust support for those in need. With concerted effort and compassion, we can create a society where mental health is acknowledged, discussed, and supported.

The Role of Community Building and Social Engagement

Loneliness is not just an individual struggle; it's a societal issue. As such, collective efforts are critical for reducing social isolation. Herein lies the power of community building and social engagement, two significant aspects that can contribute substantially to combating loneliness.

Why is Community Building Important?

Humans are inherently social creatures. We thrive in communities where we feel a sense of belonging and significance. Community building is the process of bringing people together around shared values, interests, or goals. It can act as a powerful antidote to loneliness by fostering connection, providing support, and creating opportunities for meaningful social interaction.

1. **Connection**: The sense of being part of a larger group can help individuals feel less isolated. Shared experiences and values can lead to a sense of belonging that alleviates feelings of loneliness.
2. **Support**: Communities often provide emotional, practical, and even financial support. This support network can be invaluable for individuals dealing with loneliness.
3. **Opportunities for Interaction**: Communities often host events and activities that provide an opportunity for social interaction. Participating in

these activities can help individuals forge new friendships and connections.

How to Build and Foster Community

Building and fostering a community can be a collective effort involving various stakeholders, including individuals, local government, non-profit organizations, and businesses. Here are some strategies for community building:

1. **Promote Social Cohesion**: Encourage shared experiences and collaborative projects that foster a sense of solidarity and mutual trust. This could be through neighborhood cleanup programs, local festivals, or other community events.

2. **Create Safe Spaces for Interaction**: Create public spaces like parks, community centers, or libraries that encourage social interaction. Safe, welcoming spaces can foster community engagement and participation.

3. **Leverage Technology**: Use online platforms to connect individuals with their local communities. Online communities can also be a valuable resource, particularly for those who may be housebound or live in remote areas.

The Power of Social Engagement

Social engagement refers to the act of participating in activities that involve others. This is closely tied to community building and can significantly impact reducing feelings of loneliness. Participating in social activities provides a sense of purpose, improves mental health, and cultivates connections with others.

Strategies for Encouraging Social Engagement

1. **Encourage Volunteering**: Volunteering for a local charity or organization can provide a sense of purpose and community connection. It also fosters empathy, contributing to emotional well-being.
2. **Promote Lifelong Learning**: Encourage community members to participate in adult education classes or hobby clubs. Learning something new can stimulate the brain and provide a shared interest around which connections can form.
3. **Host Community Events**: Regular community events provide an opportunity for social interaction. These could range from local farmers' markets to community theater performances or sports games.

Community building and social engagement are vital components in the battle against loneliness. They foster connection, provide support, and create opportunities for meaningful social interaction. By focusing on these areas, we can create communities where individuals feel valued and connected, reducing feelings of loneliness and isolation.

The Power of Social Support in Addressing Loneliness

The struggle with loneliness is a deeply personal one, but that does not mean one should navigate it alone. The role of social support in alleviating feelings of loneliness and social isolation is essential, and indeed, it can often be the difference between sinking under the weight of loneliness or finding the strength to rise above it. In this section, we delve into the power of social support, how it can address loneliness, and what steps we can take to ensure its availability and effectiveness.

Understanding Social Support

Social support represents the emotional and practical assistance we receive from our social network – family, friends, community members, or even professionals. It is that reassuring pat on the back when we are feeling low, the listening ear when we need to talk, the helping hand in times of need, or the shared laughter in moments of joy. Social support provides a buffer against the negative impacts of stress, including the stress that arises from feeling lonely or isolated.

The power of social support lies in its capacity to enhance our sense of self-worth, belonging, and security. It provides reassurance that we are cared for, valued, and that we belong to a network of communication and mutual obligation.

Types of Social Support

Broadly speaking, there are four types of social support:
1. **Emotional Support**: This involves showing empathy, love, trust, and caring. It includes listening, reassuring, and showing understanding and encouragement.
2. **Instrumental Support**: This is tangible aid and service that directly assist a person in need. It can be financial aid, material goods, or services.
3. **Informational Support**: This involves providing advice, suggestions, or information to help someone.
4. **Appraisal Support**: This involves information that is useful for self-evaluation, affirmation, feedback, and social comparison.

Social Support as a Buffer Against Loneliness

The buffering hypothesis suggests that social support can protect individuals from the harmful consequences of stressful events, including loneliness. By providing a buffer, social support helps us navigate challenges and boosts our resilience.

Consider an elderly individual who has lost a spouse and is dealing with loneliness. Emotional support from family members can help them process their grief and reassure them that they are not alone. Instrumental support, like assistance with daily chores or regular visits, can provide tangible help. Informational support can help them navigate their new life circumstances, and appraisal support can boost their self-esteem and sense of value.

Strategies to Enhance Social Support

1. **Nurture Existing Relationships**: Encourage the individual to invest time and effort in maintaining existing relationships. Even a simple phone call or a heartfelt conversation can enhance feelings of connectedness.
2. **Encourage New Connections**: This could involve joining clubs, attending community events, or volunteering. Shared activities and interests can provide a fertile ground for new friendships to bloom.
3. **Promote Mutual Support**: Social support should not be a one-way street. Encourage individuals to provide support to others as well. This not only strengthens the bonds of friendship but also enhances self-esteem and feelings of self-worth.
4. **Leverage Technology**: Online platforms can provide valuable support, particularly for individuals who may be housebound or geographically isolated. Online forums, social media platforms, and virtual support groups can provide a sense of community and belonging.

Social support is a powerful tool in the battle against loneliness. By fostering connection and a sense of belonging, it can alleviate feelings of isolation. It is incumbent upon all of us – individuals, communities, and societies – to ensure that social support is available and accessible to those who need it.

After all, the burden of loneliness is lighter when shared.

Chapter 9: Global Perspectives and Innovative Solutions to Loneliness

Loneliness Around the World: Cross-Cultural Experiences and Approaches

It is a common misconception that loneliness is a homogeneous, universal phenomenon that affects everyone in the same manner. The reality is that while the experience of loneliness is a shared human condition, its manifestation and the coping mechanisms employed can vary significantly across different cultures. A globally inclusive approach to combating loneliness therefore requires us to understand these diverse experiences and apply that understanding in the creation of innovative solutions.

Cultural Interpretations of Loneliness

Loneliness is a deeply subjective experience, and one that is often framed by cultural norms and expectations. How individuals perceive, experience, and express loneliness can be significantly influenced by their cultural background.

In some cultures, admitting to feelings of loneliness can be perceived as a sign of weakness or failure, thus creating a stigma around the topic. For example, in societies with an emphasis on individualism like the United States, feelings of loneliness may be seen as a personal failure to establish successful social relationships. On the other hand, in collectivist societies like Japan, loneliness can be perceived as a failure of the social network to provide adequate companionship.

Cross-Cultural Approaches to Addressing Loneliness

The way societies approach loneliness and isolation can also vary greatly. Some cultures encourage community participation and intergenerational living arrangements to reduce isolation. Others have community activities and programs designed to engage individuals and foster social connections.

For instance, in Scandinavian countries known for their robust social welfare systems, a variety of programs such as community centres and recreational activities are offered to foster social connections, especially among the elderly. In contrast, countries like India with its joint family system often relies on familial bonds and responsibilities to mitigate feelings of loneliness.

Innovative Solutions to Loneliness

Appreciating the cultural nuances in the experiences and interpretations of loneliness allows for the development of more effective and culturally sensitive solutions. These can range from policy-level interventions, community-based initiatives, to individual-level strategies.

At a policy level, governments can initiate social programs designed to engage individuals, create community connections, and facilitate access to mental health resources. For example, the United Kingdom appointed a Minister for Loneliness in 2018 to tackle the issue head-on at a national level.

Community-based initiatives can foster engagement and connection, as seen in examples like the "Men's Sheds" in Australia, where men come together to work on projects, thereby reducing social isolation. Similarly, intergenerational living programs, such as those in the Netherlands, offer students free accommodation in elderly care homes in exchange for spending time with the residents.

Individual-level strategies can include psychological interventions, including cognitive behavioural therapy (CBT), which can help individuals change negative thought patterns contributing to feelings of loneliness.

Understanding loneliness from a global perspective is crucial in developing effective, holistic, and culturally sensitive strategies to combat it. By learning from different cultural contexts, we can innovate and adapt solutions to better address the loneliness epidemic in its many manifestations.

Innovative Community Initiatives Combatting Loneliness

As we have navigated the terrain of understanding and addressing loneliness, we have come to acknowledge the profound role that community plays in our social lives. This chapter illuminates various innovative community initiatives worldwide that have been successful in mitigating loneliness. As we explore these endeavors, we aim to inspire readers to take active roles in their communities or even spearhead similar initiatives in their locales.

Creating Connections through Shared Interests

One of the most effective ways to combat loneliness is by fostering a sense of belonging and connection. Initiatives that revolve around shared interests or hobbies have proven to be particularly successful in this regard. For example, the "Men's Sheds" initiative in Australia serves as a communal space for men to share tools and work on projects, typically involving woodworking, metalworking, and other manual arts. By creating a space for mutual support, camaraderie, and shared productivity, these sheds have been pivotal in tackling loneliness among men, particularly the elderly.

Similar to "Men's Sheds," the "Repair Cafes" initiative, originating in the Netherlands but now spread worldwide, invites people to bring in their broken items to be repaired by volunteers. These cafes not only encourage sustainability but also foster social connections among participants and volunteers.

Empowering Individuals through Volunteering

Research has consistently shown that helping others can significantly alleviate feelings of loneliness. Volunteering provides individuals with a sense of purpose and facilitates social connections. This is the core principle of initiatives like "The Campaign to End Loneliness" in the UK, which urges people to take simple actions to help others, like checking on a neighbor or starting a conversation with someone in their community.

In a more formalized structure, organizations like "Volunteer Grandparents" in Canada pair seniors with families who lack grandparental support. Through this intergenerational exchange, seniors can contribute to their communities, while also forming meaningful bonds.

Leveraging Technology to Build Communities

Technology, often blamed for increasing isolation, can also be part of the solution if used wisely. Several initiatives use technology to combat loneliness by building virtual communities. The "ChatGPT Community" is one such initiative, using AI technology to provide companionship and interaction for those who may be isolated or housebound.

Moreover, apps like "MeetUp" allow people to create and join groups of like-minded individuals who share common interests, from book clubs to hiking groups. These platforms facilitate face-to-face interactions, which can lead to sustained connections.

Integrating Community Services

Integrating community services, such as libraries, parks, and recreation centers, into the fight against loneliness is another effective approach. For instance, the "Healthy Libraries" program in New York promotes libraries as hubs for health information and activities. With activities ranging from yoga classes to cooking demonstrations, the program leverages existing community infrastructure to promote social interaction.

Lessons and Implications

The innovative community initiatives highlighted in this chapter underscore that the fight against loneliness is multifaceted, requiring a range of approaches. While every community has its unique needs, these examples provide a blueprint of what can be achieved.

As a reader, you can draw inspiration from these examples to either participate in similar initiatives in your community or to launch new ones. Whether it's starting a book club, organizing a local repair cafe, or volunteering at a local charity, every action counts in the fight against loneliness. Remember, in addressing your loneliness, you could also be helping someone else overcome theirs.

In the battle against the loneliness epidemic, our strongest weapon is community. By fostering a sense of belonging and mutual support within our neighborhoods, we not only mitigate loneliness but also build stronger, more resilient societies.

Revolutionary Digital Platforms and Therapies for Loneliness

In today's digital age, innovative platforms and technologies have become an integral part of the conversation around loneliness. These tools can not only help people feel more connected but also provide therapeutic benefits. In this chapter, we delve into the revolutionary digital platforms and therapies that are transforming the landscape of loneliness interventions.

Harnessing the Power of Social Media

While social media often gets blamed for contributing to loneliness and isolation, when used appropriately, it can also be a powerful tool to combat loneliness. For instance, platforms like Facebook and Instagram allow people to stay connected with family and friends, even when they are physically distant. Additionally, they provide a platform for people to join groups based on shared interests or experiences, fostering a sense of community and belonging.

However, it's essential to approach social media mindfully, focusing on meaningful connections and avoiding comparisons or excessive screen time. A solution could be to use apps that limit daily screen time or notify you when you spend too much time on certain apps.

Virtual Reality: A New Frontier in Loneliness Intervention

Virtual reality (VR) has been making significant strides in loneliness therapy. VR can immerse users in a three-dimensional environment, providing a sense of presence that can alleviate feelings of loneliness.

One promising example is the use of VR for social therapy. Apps such as "vTime XR" allow users to create avatars and meet in virtual spaces, from a luxurious yacht to a lunar landscape. This can be particularly beneficial for individuals with mobility issues, allowing them to socialize without leaving their homes.

Additionally, VR has shown potential in therapeutic settings. Guided VR meditation, for instance, can provide a calming, immersive experience that can help manage stress and anxiety associated with loneliness.

Artificial Intelligence: The Future of Companionship?

Artificial Intelligence (AI) has opened a new avenue in addressing loneliness, especially through chatbots. These AI-powered software systems can simulate human conversation, providing a constant, non-judgmental companion for those feeling lonely.

One notable example is the AI "Replika," designed to become a 'personal AI friend.' The more you talk to Replika, the more it learns about you, allowing it to provide more personalized and meaningful interactions. While it does not replace human relationships, it can provide comfort and companionship when one feels isolated.

Teletherapy: Therapy from the Comfort of Your Home

With the rise of telecommunication technologies, mental health services have become more accessible than ever. Teletherapy platforms like "Talkspace" and "BetterHelp" provide online counseling services, allowing individuals to communicate with certified therapists via text, voice, or video call. This can be especially helpful for those who feel lonely but find it difficult to seek help in-person due to stigma, accessibility issues, or social anxiety.

Digital Platforms for Skill Building and Personal Development

Platforms such as "Meetup" or "Eventbrite" allow people to find local groups or events based on their interests, providing opportunities for socializing and skill building. Additionally, learning platforms like "Coursera" or "MasterClass" not only allow individuals to engage in personal development but also connect with others with similar learning interests.

East vs. West: A Different Lens on Loneliness

Western societies, with their emphasis on individualism and self-reliance, often view loneliness as a personal issue, a result of individual circumstances or psychological conditions. Eastern societies, however, with their focus on community and collective welfare, often perceive loneliness more as a societal issue, stemming from the inability of the community or society to provide individuals with a sense of belonging.

Take, for example, Japan's approach to tackling loneliness, a country where the number of older adults living alone has been steadily rising. The government has recently appointed a 'Minister of Loneliness' to address the escalating rates of social isolation among the elderly. The plan focuses on community outreach and social participation programs to reconnect older adults with their communities. It's a perspective that frames loneliness not as an individual failure, but as a societal one.

Digital Solutions Across the Globe

Across the world, digital solutions are being innovatively used to combat loneliness. In the UK, an app called 'MindMate' provides cognitive stimulation for seniors, while also allowing them to share stories and make connections with others, combining cognitive health with social connection.

India has taken a multi-generational approach, with the 'My Saheli' app, which connects younger women with older women in their communities, fostering mentorship, companionship, and shared experiences. And in the United States, 'Nextdoor', a social networking app for neighborhoods, encourages community building and local connection to reduce feelings of isolation.

Therapeutic Approaches: A Worldwide Overview

Cognitive-Behavioral Therapy (CBT) has shown great promise in tackling loneliness across various cultural contexts. In countries like Australia and Canada, CBT, often combined with mindfulness-based stress reduction techniques, is used to help individuals understand and change negative thought patterns that can exacerbate feelings of loneliness.

Other countries lean towards community-based approaches. In Denmark, the concept of 'folkekokken', or 'people's kitchen', promotes community dinners that bring together people of all ages, reducing social isolation and strengthening community bonds. In Brazil, 'Roda de Conversa', or 'conversation circles', are regularly organized in neighborhoods, promoting open community dialogue about various issues, including loneliness and social isolation.

Understanding the strategies and interventions used across the globe can provide us with a broad toolbox of techniques to deal with loneliness, adapted to the local cultural context. The approaches vary, but the objective remains the same: to connect people, foster a sense of belonging, and create supportive, resilient communities where loneliness can't easily take root.

Creating Virtual Communities

The rise of social media platforms has certainly been a double-edged sword. On one hand, it has led to concerns about superficial connections, online bullying, and other mental health issues. On the other hand, it has made it possible to connect with like-minded individuals across geographical boundaries, fostering a sense of community that might not be available in one's immediate physical environment.

Take, for example, the platform 'Meetup'. This online platform allows people to create and join groups based on common interests, ranging from hiking, to book clubs, to coding. Meetups are organized within local communities, ensuring that online interactions can lead to face-to-face connections. This can be especially valuable for individuals who feel isolated due to unique hobbies or interests not shared by their immediate circle.

The Role of Apps

There are also a number of mobile applications specifically designed to help people combat loneliness. Apps such as 'TalkLife', for instance, provide a platform where individuals struggling with loneliness and other mental health issues can connect, share their experiences, and provide support to each other in a safe, moderated environment.

For those who might be wary of opening up to strangers, 'Woebot', an AI-powered chatbot, uses principles from cognitive behavioral therapy to provide an interactive form of self-help. It checks in with users daily, providing exercises and insights to improve mental health.

Online Therapies and Interventions

Online therapies and interventions are another innovative solution. A range of services are available, from apps that provide self-help tools based on cognitive-behavioral therapy principles, to platforms that connect users with qualified therapists for video or text-based sessions.

Take 'BetterHelp', for example. This platform offers online counselling services, allowing individuals to connect with professional therapists via message, live chat, phone, or video. The service provides the benefit of traditional therapy without the limitations of location and scheduling, making it more accessible to those who might otherwise be unable to seek help.

Combating Loneliness Through Gaming

Gaming is another area where digital platforms are being used to combat loneliness. Massively multiplayer online games (MMOGs) such as 'World of Warcraft' allow players to connect, collaborate, and build communities in virtual worlds. For many, these gaming communities can provide a sense of belonging and camaraderie that they may struggle to find in the physical world.

Digital Platforms for Seniors

Finally, it's worth noting that digital platforms can play a crucial role in combatting loneliness among seniors, a demographic particularly prone to social isolation. Platforms such as 'SeniorChatters' provide a safe, moderated space where older adults can chat, share experiences, and build friendships.

Looking Forward

While digital platforms are not a panacea for loneliness, they offer innovative and accessible solutions for individuals who may otherwise struggle to make connections. As we continue to navigate the digital age, it is essential to harness the connective potential of these platforms and use them to build communities, foster engagement, and provide resources for those struggling with loneliness.

However, just as important is the need for safeguards to ensure these platforms are used responsibly and do not contribute to the very issue they aim to solve. With a thoughtful, balanced approach, digital technology can serve as a powerful tool in the fight against the loneliness epidemic.

Innovative Approaches for Tomorrow

In our fight against the global loneliness epidemic, innovation, creativity, and a willingness to learn from each other's experiences are our greatest allies. From digital platforms to government initiatives, from cognitive therapies to community-building strategies, solutions to loneliness are as diverse as humanity itself. And while there's no 'one-size-fits-all' answer, these varied approaches, grounded in empathy and understanding, bring us closer to a world where loneliness is the exception, not the norm.

As we strive to understand loneliness, we must never forget that it's our shared human experiences, our universal desire for connection and belonging, that will ultimately guide us towards innovative, effective solutions.

In this journey, no one is alone.

Chapter 10: Personal Tools and Techniques to Combat Loneliness

Developing Emotional Intelligence and Resilience

Loneliness can strike anyone, anywhere, at any point in their life. It's a common human experience that transcends age, gender, and geography. But despite its universality, it is often accompanied by a unique sense of isolation. This chapter will delve into how the development of emotional intelligence and resilience can provide us with personal tools and techniques to combat loneliness.

Understanding Emotional Intelligence

Emotional intelligence (EQ), as first introduced by psychologists Peter Salovey and John D. Mayer, and later popularized by Daniel Goleman, refers to the ability to identify, use, understand, and manage emotions in positive ways. It impacts many different aspects of our daily lives, including our ability to manage stress, communicate effectively, empathize with others, overcome challenges, and defuse conflict.

People with high EQ can better identify and control their own emotions, which can lead to more peaceful and fulfilling relationships with others. They are also better able to understand the feelings of others, which is a vital aspect of forming strong connections and combating loneliness.

To develop your EQ, start by observing your emotions without judgment, identifying the triggers that lead to certain emotional responses. Mindfulness and meditation can be particularly helpful in cultivating this awareness. Practicing empathetic listening and response can also aid in building emotional intelligence. By seeking to understand before being understood, we can create a more profound connection with others.

The Role of Resilience

Resilience, another key aspect of combatting loneliness, is the ability to recover from setbacks, adapt well to change, and keep going in the face of adversity. Resilient individuals do not let hardship or dramatic change derail them. Instead, they manage to find a way to move forward and continue growing.

Resilience does not eliminate stress or erase life's difficulties. People who possess this resilience don't see life through rose-colored glasses. They understand that setbacks happen and sometimes life is hard and unfair. However, they have developed the capacity to rise above these challenges and forge a path forward.

Building resilience requires a positive mindset and problem-solving skills. Being proactive in managing your mental health, such as seeking help when necessary, is a crucial part of this. Additionally, maintaining physical health through regular exercise, a healthy diet, and adequate sleep can contribute to overall resilience.

Connecting Emotional Intelligence and Resilience

Emotional intelligence and resilience go hand in hand. High EQ can help manage stress and navigate emotional challenges, contributing to greater resilience. Similarly, being resilient in the face of adversity can enhance emotional intelligence by fostering a deeper understanding of our emotions and how they impact our actions and interactions.

Combating loneliness requires a multifaceted approach. Emotional intelligence and resilience are just two aspects of a larger toolkit. It's also essential to reach out to others, engage in activities that bring joy and meaning, and seek professional help when needed.

As we journey through this chapter and the chapters ahead, remember that loneliness is a common human experience. It's okay to feel lonely and to ask for help. And while these feelings can be overwhelming, they are also a reminder of our inherent need for connection.

It's this very need that makes us human, and through understanding and managing our emotions and building resilience, we can navigate the challenges of loneliness and build a more connected, fulfilling life.

Mindfulness and Meditation: Inner Connection as a Pathway to Social Connection

One of the many paradoxes of human nature is that we can feel lonely even when surrounded by others. At the heart of this is a profound disconnection – not only from those around us but also from ourselves. This chapter will explore how mindfulness and meditation, two practices deeply rooted in connecting us to our internal experiences, can be key allies in our quest to build healthier social connections and combat loneliness.

Understanding Mindfulness

Let's start with mindfulness, a term that's gained considerable traction in the contemporary lexicon but is often misunderstood. Mindfulness is a state of open, non-judgmental, and focused attention on the present moment. It's about fully engaging with here and now, not getting lost in regrets about the past or anxieties about the future. It invites us to experience life as it unfolds, in all its richness and complexity.

The Role of Meditation

Meditation is a systematic practice that develops mindfulness. It involves focusing our attention and eliminating the stream of jumbled thoughts that may be crowding our minds. Done consistently, meditation leads to a state of relaxation and tranquil mind. While there are various forms of meditation, from breath-focused to loving-kindness meditation, they all aim to cultivate a greater awareness and understanding of life.

Inner Connection: The First Step to Outer Connection

Now, you may ask, how does focusing on the self-help address a problem that seemingly arises from insufficient connection with others? The answer lies in the realization that genuine connection with others begins with a genuine connection with ourselves.

By cultivating awareness of our thoughts and feelings, mindfulness and meditation help us understand ourselves better. This self-understanding is the foundation of self-acceptance, and ultimately, self-love. As we become more comfortable in our skin, we also become less reliant on others for validation. This self-reliance forms the basis of healthier relationships, wherein we engage with others for mutual growth rather than out of desperate neediness.

Mindfulness and Empathy

Mindfulness also enhances our capacity for empathy, the ability to understand and share the feelings of others. When we're present, we're more attuned to the feelings and needs of others, allowing us to respond with greater sensitivity. This deeper level of understanding can significantly improve the quality of our relationships, making us feel more connected and less lonely.

Practical Mindfulness and Meditation Techniques

So, how can we integrate mindfulness and meditation into our lives? Here are a few practical tips:

1. **Start small:** If you're new to meditation, start with short, manageable sessions – even a few minutes can make a difference. Over time, as you get more comfortable, you can gradually lengthen your meditation sessions.
2. **Make it a habit:** Consistency is key when it comes to mindfulness and meditation. Make them part of your daily routine. It could be in the morning to start your day with a calm mind, or at night to wind down.
3. **Focus on your breath:** Your breath is a powerful anchor that can bring you back to the present moment. Whenever you notice that your mind has wandered, gently bring your attention back to your breath.

4. **Practice mindful listening:** This involves fully focusing on the other person and trying to understand their perspective, without interrupting or planning your response. It not only makes the other person feel valued but also facilitates deeper connections.

5. **Be patient with yourself:** Mindfulness and meditation are skills that take time to develop. You're bound to have sessions where your mind wanders incessantly. That's perfectly okay. The aim is not to empty your mind but to notice where your mind goes and gently guide it back to the present moment.

By cultivating an inner connection, mindfulness and meditation can be powerful tools to combat the epidemic of loneliness. Remember, the journey out of loneliness is not about filling our lives with people; it's about deepening our connections, starting with the one with ourselves.

Fostering Genuine Connections: Communication in a Digital Age

In the contemporary era, we live in a global village where digital technologies have significantly redefined communication. The internet and smartphones bring distant places and people within our reach at the click of a button. However, the paradox of our age is that despite being hyper-connected digitally, many individuals experience profound loneliness. This chapter explores the concept of fostering genuine connections in the digital age, offering readers actionable insights and solutions to combat loneliness and isolation in the modern world.

Understanding the Digital Age

To effectively address loneliness in the digital age, we must first understand the unique characteristics of this era. The digital age, also known as the information age, is marked by the rapid transition from traditional industry established by the industrial revolution to an economy primarily based upon information technology.

The advent of social media platforms, online forums, video call apps, and messaging services has enabled instant and constant communication. Theoretically, this should make us feel more connected than ever. However, many individuals feel alienated and isolated, with superficial online interactions often replacing deeper, face-to-face connections.

The Paradox of Connection and Isolation

Today, we can have hundreds, even thousands, of friends on Facebook, followers on Instagram, or connections on LinkedIn, but does that make us feel more connected? Not necessarily. Studies have shown that spending too much time on social media can increase feelings of loneliness and depression. Online interactions, while valuable and often enjoyable, can be impersonal and lack the emotional warmth, non-verbal cues, and nuances that enrich face-to-face communication.

The digital age presents us with a paradox: while we are more connected than ever in terms of quantity, the quality of our connections is often lacking. The challenge lies in leveraging digital communication tools to foster genuine, meaningful connections that can mitigate feelings of loneliness.

Strategies for Fostering Genuine Connections

Here are some strategies that can help you establish deeper connections and counter loneliness in this digital age:

1. **Digital Detox:** Consider taking regular breaks from digital devices to reduce screen time. While technology is a powerful tool, disconnecting from the digital world periodically can improve mental health and open opportunities for real-life interactions.

2. **Quality over Quantity:** It's more beneficial to have deep, meaningful conversations with a few friends than superficial interactions with a large number of acquaintances. Try to foster quality connections both online and offline.

3. **Express Authenticity:** Be your authentic self online. Authenticity breeds connection. Share your experiences, thoughts, and feelings honestly. This

encourages others to do the same, fostering genuine connections.

4. **Mindful Communication:** Be present in your interactions, whether they're online or offline. Listen actively and empathetically. This demonstrates to the other person that you value their thoughts and feelings, deepening your connection with them.

5. **Use Technology Mindfully:** Leverage technology to enhance rather than replace real-world interactions. Use video calls to stay in touch with distant friends and family, join online communities that share your interests, or use digital platforms to organize real-world meetups.

6. **Be Proactive:** Don't wait for others to reach out. Make the first move. Start a conversation, organize a meet-up, or simply check in with a friend to see how they're doing.

7. **Seek Professional Help:** If feelings of loneliness persist, don't hesitate to seek help from a mental health professional. They can provide strategies tailored to your specific situation and needs.

Wrapping Up

Fostering genuine connections in the digital age is a challenge that many individuals grapple with. It's crucial to remember that technology is just a tool. The onus is on us to use it wisely to augment our social connections and not let it replace the warmth and comfort of real-world interactions.

We're living in an era of unprecedented connectedness, yet loneliness is a pervasive issue. By understanding the dynamics of communication in the digital age and implementing strategies to foster authentic connections, we can make headway in combating the loneliness epidemic. Remember, a digital age doesn't have to mean a lonely age. With mindfulness and effort, we can utilize the tools of the digital age to foster genuine connections and reduce feelings of loneliness and isolation.

Developing Effective Communication Skills for Stronger Relationships

Communication, the process of exchanging information or conveying thoughts and feelings, is the lifeblood of any relationship. It bridges the gap between individuals and helps to build and maintain connections. Yet, in a world increasingly dominated by digital technologies, cultivating effective communication skills can pose a significant challenge. This chapter seeks to unravel the importance of honing these skills and provides practical strategies to enhance them, which in turn, can help to alleviate feelings of loneliness and establish stronger relationships.

Understanding the Importance of Communication

Before diving into strategies, it's crucial to underscore why communication is pivotal. Effective communication fosters understanding, boosts empathy, resolves conflicts, and strengthens emotional connections. It allows us to express our needs and concerns and to comprehend those of others. Yet, the ability to communicate effectively does not come naturally to all of us, but is a skill that can be developed and refined over time.

The Art of Listening

Active listening forms the bedrock of effective communication. The act of listening goes beyond merely hearing the words spoken. It involves understanding the message being conveyed, recognizing the emotions behind the words, and responding appropriately.

To become an active listener, avoid distractions when someone is speaking to you. Give them your full attention, maintain eye contact, and provide verbal and non-verbal feedback. Be empathetic and open-minded. Refrain from formulating your response while they're still speaking. This enables you to fully grasp what they're communicating.

The Power of Non-Verbal Communication

Non-verbal cues such as facial expressions, gestures, body posture, and tone of voice often communicate more than words. They reflect our true feelings and attitudes. By becoming aware of and adept at interpreting these cues, we can enhance our communication effectiveness.

Mind your body language when interacting with others. Maintain an open posture, make eye contact, and ensure your facial expressions and tone align with your words. Similarly, observe others' non-verbal cues to gauge their emotions and responses.

Expressing Yourself Clearly and Assertively

Clarity and assertiveness are key components of effective communication. Clarity ensures your message is understood as intended, while assertiveness enables you to express your thoughts and feelings honestly and respectfully.

To communicate clearly, organize your thoughts before you speak, use simple and concise language, and confirm the listener's understanding. To be assertive, express your needs and feelings directly, use "I" statements to own your emotions, and respect the rights and feelings of others.

Managing Conflicts Constructively

Conflicts are inevitable in any relationship. However, effective communication can transform conflicts into opportunities for growth and understanding.

To manage conflicts constructively, listen to the other person's perspective without interrupting, express your viewpoint without blaming or criticizing, focus on the issue at hand instead of resorting to personal attacks, and seek a compromise that respects both parties' needs and feelings.

The Role of Emotional Intelligence

Emotional intelligence, the ability to understand, manage, and effectively express one's own feelings, as well as engage and navigate successfully with those of others, is integral to effective communication. It enables us to empathize with others, manage our emotions in stressful situations, and resolve conflicts amicably.

To enhance your emotional intelligence, practice self-awareness by recognizing your emotions and their impact on your behavior. Develop self-management skills to regulate your emotions, especially in stressful situations. Practice empathy to understand others' feelings, and hone your social skills to interact effectively with others.

Applying Communication Skills in the Digital Age

In the digital age, much of our communication happens through digital channels. Here, the principles of effective communication still apply, but they take on new dimensions.

In online interactions, clarity becomes even more crucial as we lack the non-verbal cues available in face-to-face conversations. Ensure your messages are clear and concise, use emoticons to convey tone, and be mindful of your digital etiquette.

Moreover, active listening in the digital sphere involves fully engaging with the content someone shares, providing thoughtful responses, and asking clarifying questions. Being attentive to the choice of words, tone, and context can help deduce the emotions behind digital messages.

Developing effective communication skills is a lifelong journey, not a destination. It requires continual practice, self-reflection, and the willingness to learn and adapt. As we enhance these skills, we're not only improving our relationships but also taking steps to combat loneliness. Remember, at the heart of every interaction is the desire to connect, understand, and be understood. By fostering effective communication, we can satisfy this inherent need, creating stronger, more fulfilling relationships.

Self-help Strategies for Overcoming Loneliness

Loneliness can be a complex emotional experience, often exacerbated by our thoughts and responses to perceived isolation. While professional help can be invaluable in some cases, there are also several self-help strategies that can assist us in overcoming feelings of loneliness. This section will explore some of these strategies that have been found to be effective in combating loneliness, enabling readers to navigate their journey towards greater connection with confidence.

Understanding Loneliness

Understanding loneliness is the first step towards overcoming it. Loneliness is a universal human experience, an emotional response to perceived isolation or a lack of connection with others. It's essential to remember that feeling lonely does not mean you're alone or unloved. It's a signal that you need more social connection, not a reflection of your worth or likability.

Maintaining a Healthy Lifestyle

A healthy lifestyle can play a vital role in alleviating feelings of loneliness. Regular physical activity, a balanced diet, adequate sleep, and abstinence from alcohol, nicotine, or drugs can boost your mood, increase energy levels, improve sleep, and reduce stress. Moreover, taking care of your physical health can also enhance your self-esteem and confidence, promoting positive social interactions.

Practicing Mindfulness and Meditation

Mindfulness and meditation can be powerful tools in combating loneliness. They involve focusing on the present moment and accepting it without judgment. This focus can help reduce rumination and negative thinking associated with loneliness. Regular practice can also increase self-awareness, promoting understanding of your feelings and enabling better management of loneliness.

Fostering Connections

Building and maintaining social connections is one of the most effective ways to combat loneliness. Reach out to family, friends, or neighbors. Engage in social activities that interest you. Volunteering or joining a club or community group can provide opportunities to connect with others and build new friendships.

Improving Communication Skills

Effective communication can help deepen existing relationships and establish new ones. Active listening, expressing yourself clearly and assertively, understanding non-verbal cues, managing conflicts constructively, and developing emotional intelligence are all part of effective communication. These skills can be cultivated and enhanced with practice.

Developing Self-compassion

Self-compassion involves treating oneself with kindness, recognizing one's shared humanity, and being mindful when considering negative aspects of oneself. Cultivating self-compassion can help you manage negative emotions associated with loneliness and foster a healthier relationship with yourself.

Seeking Professional Help

While self-help strategies can be effective, professional help may be necessary for persistent or overwhelming loneliness. A mental health professional can provide strategies to manage loneliness and address any underlying issues, such as depression or anxiety. Don't hesitate to reach out to a professional if you're struggling.

Adopting a Positive Outlook

Your thoughts and attitudes can significantly impact how you experience loneliness. Adopting a positive outlook, focusing on your strengths, expressing gratitude, and practicing positive self-talk can enhance your resilience and ability to cope with loneliness.

Overcoming loneliness is a journey that requires patience, courage, and perseverance. These self-help strategies can be invaluable tools along this path. Yet, remember that it's okay to ask for help and lean on others. You're not alone in your feelings of loneliness, and with time and effort, you can build a fulfilling, connected life.

We are social beings, and it's natural for us to yearn for connection. In times when loneliness strikes, these strategies can help navigate the terrain of isolation and move toward a space of connection and belonging. A space where we can not only exist but thrive.

Chapter 11: The Influence of Urban Design in Combatting Loneliness

The Role of Urban Planning in Promoting or Limiting Social Connection

As we navigate through the chapters of The Loneliness Epidemic, we continue to broaden our understanding of this complex issue. We've discussed personal strategies and emotional intelligence, and now we venture into the realm of urban design and its role in promoting or limiting social connection.

Urban design, at its core, is about creating spaces that accommodate the diverse needs of a population. It involves the configuration and arrangement of buildings, public spaces, transport systems, services, and amenities. It's a multidimensional process that impacts how we live, interact, and connect with each other and our environment.

How Urban Design Impacts Loneliness

There's an old saying: "We shape our buildings; thereafter, they shape us." This notion applies not only to individual structures but also to the layout of our cities. Urban design can profoundly affect our social interactions. It can bring us together, creating vibrant, connected communities, or it can separate us, leading to isolation and loneliness.

Urban environments that lack spaces for social interaction – such as parks, community centers, and pedestrian-friendly streets – can contribute to feelings of loneliness and isolation. Conversely, urban design that encourages interaction, such as well-planned public spaces, community gardens, and 'complete streets' that are designed to be accessible to all users (pedestrians, cyclists, motorists, and transit riders), can foster a sense of community and help combat loneliness.

Urban Planning: An Unexpected Tool

The role of urban planning in this context might seem unexpected. But think about it. How many times have you bumped into a friend at the local park, started a conversation with a stranger at a coffee shop, or bonded with neighbors during a street festival? These spontaneous interactions, often made possible by thoughtful urban design, play a crucial role in building strong, connected communities.

Urban planning can also combat loneliness by promoting inclusivity. By ensuring that urban spaces are accessible to people of all ages, abilities, and socio-economic backgrounds, we can foster an environment where everyone feels welcomed and connected.

City Living and Loneliness: The Paradox

Interestingly, while cities offer numerous opportunities for social interaction, city dwellers often report feeling lonely. This paradox may be due to several factors, including high population density, socio-economic disparities, and the anonymity that city life can sometimes confer.

Moreover, the hustle and bustle of city life can lead to 'aloneness by choice,' where individuals, overwhelmed by the surrounding stimulus, retreat into their shells. This makes the role of urban design in creating 'breathing spaces' where people can connect on a human scale even more critical.

Designing for Connection

So, how can we use urban design to combat loneliness? Here are a few strategies:

1. **Create Social Spaces**: Public spaces like parks, plazas, and community centers can serve as social hubs, encouraging spontaneous interaction.
2. **Prioritize Walkability**: Pedestrian-friendly streets promote interaction between residents, foster a sense of community, and increase opportunities for social contact.
3. **Ensure Accessibility**: Urban spaces should be accessible to all individuals, regardless of their physical ability or age. This includes having wheelchair-accessible buildings and streets, well-lit paths, and benches for rest.

4. **Promote Mixed-Use Development**: Encourage a mix of residential, commercial, and recreational use within neighborhoods. This approach fosters a sense of community and reduces the need for long commutes, providing more opportunities for social interaction.

5. **Incorporate Nature**: Access to green spaces has been linked to improved mental health. Parks, community gardens, and tree-lined streets can offer peaceful retreats from the urban hustle and bustle.

6. **Encourage Community Involvement in Planning Process**: When community members are actively involved in the planning process, they're more likely to feel a sense of ownership and connection to their neighborhood.

Loneliness is an issue that can permeate every aspect of our lives – even down to the design of our cities. However, by using urban planning and design as tools to promote social connection, we can create environments that foster community and combat the loneliness epidemic. Urban design, therefore, becomes a social issue, not just an aesthetic one, a solution in our collective toolbox to tackle the modern crisis of social isolation.

Successful City Designs that Foster Social Connections

While the previous chapter offered an overview of how urban design can combat loneliness by promoting social connection, let's delve further into this topic by examining successful city designs that foster such connections. These real-world examples will provide us with a concrete idea of how urban planning, executed thoughtfully, can have a positive impact on our social health and well-being.

Copenhagen, Denmark: Embracing Cycling and Pedestrianization

Copenhagen is often hailed as one of the world's most livable cities, and for good reason. Its commitment to creating a city for people, not just cars, is evident in its infrastructure. With over 60% of trips in the city being made by bike, Copenhagen's urban design promotes an active lifestyle, social interaction, and environmental sustainability. The city has numerous parks and public spaces, and its popular waterfront is a lively hub of activity, encouraging residents and visitors alike to connect and socialize.

Barcelona, Spain: The Superblocks Initiative

The Superblocks project in Barcelona is another bold example of city design fostering social connections. These blocks, or 'superilles' in Catalan, are grid-like zones where traffic is minimized, and public spaces are maximized. Inside a superblock, the speed limit is significantly reduced, and the majority of the space is dedicated to pedestrians and recreational activities. The result is a quieter, safer, and cleaner environment that encourages community interaction and connection.

Curitiba, Brazil: Rapid Bus Transit System

Curitiba's Rapid Bus Transit system is a shining example of how transport can influence social connection. Introduced in the 1970s, it was designed to be an affordable, efficient, and comprehensive public transport system that would encourage people to leave their cars at home. The system's success lies in its simplicity and accessibility, fostering a sense of community among riders and reducing the isolation that can come with car-dependent lifestyles.

Portland, USA: Neighborhood Greenways and Public Spaces

In Portland, Oregon, the city's "20-minute neighborhoods" initiative aims to create vibrant, walkable communities where residents can access most of their daily needs within a 20-minute walk. The initiative is complemented by the development of Neighborhood Greenways – residential streets with low speeds where pedestrians and cyclists have priority. Together, these efforts aim to reduce car dependency, improve physical health, and foster community ties.

Singapore: Mixed-Use Developments and Green Spaces

Singapore, a city-state with limited land and a high population density, has turned to mixed-use developments and the integration of green spaces as a solution to foster social connection. One example is the Tampines Eco Green park, a unique area that has been left largely untouched, allowing visitors to experience the area's natural ecosystems. It's a tranquil space that serves as a community meeting point and a haven from the bustling city.

Key Takeaways: Planning for People

What these examples show us is that successful city design puts people first. Whether it's creating safe and accessible transport systems, promoting walkability, developing mixed-use neighborhoods, or integrating green spaces, the common thread is designing with the community's needs in mind.

Of course, it's essential to remember that what works for one city might not work for another. The local culture, climate, geography, and other factors play a crucial role in determining the most effective strategies. Community involvement in the planning process can ensure that these strategies are tailored to the community's unique needs and desires.

By studying these successful examples, we can draw inspiration for designing our own communities in ways that foster social connections and combat loneliness.

Future Cities: Designing Urban Spaces with Connection in Mind

Let's embark on a journey into the future, exploring the new frontier of urban design that takes social connection into consideration. The vision of future cities isn't merely about towering skyscrapers, smart homes, and autonomous vehicles. Instead, it's about designing inclusive urban spaces that foster social bonds, build community, and alleviate the scourge of loneliness.

Urban Design: Beyond Infrastructure

Urban design is more than just the layout and aesthetics of a city; it's about creating spaces that promote social equity, mental well-being, and strong community bonds. But how do we go about this? How do we build cities of the future that are not only functional and aesthetically pleasing but also vibrant with social connection? Here are some key considerations.

1. People-Centered Planning

Future cities should prioritize people, not cars. The key is to design cities where essential services and amenities are within walking or cycling distance, reducing the reliance on cars. This concept of 15-minute cities, similar to the initiative in Portland we discussed in the previous chapter, fosters community connection and supports local businesses.

2. Mixed-Use Spaces

Mixed-use spaces that combine residential, commercial, and recreational uses in one area can create vibrant communities where people can live, work, and play. These spaces encourage interaction among residents and create a sense of belonging and community.

3. Incorporating Nature

Cities of the future must seamlessly incorporate green spaces into their design. Parks, gardens, and even vertical forests on buildings can provide residents with a much-needed connection to nature, improving mental health and fostering social interactions.

4. Flexible Public Spaces

Public spaces should be versatile and adaptable, able to host a range of activities such as markets, festivals, sports, or just casual gatherings. By creating spaces that cater to various interests and activities, cities can promote diverse social interactions.

5. Prioritizing Accessibility

Future cities should be designed to be inclusive and accessible for everyone, regardless of age, mobility, or socioeconomic status. This includes ensuring public transportation is accessible, creating safe pedestrian paths, and ensuring public spaces are welcoming to everyone.

6. Harnessing Technology

While we must be careful not to let technology isolate us further, we can harness it to improve urban design. Smart cities, powered by data and technology, can be more responsive to their residents' needs, improving everything from traffic flow to public safety.

Future Cities in Action

Several cities worldwide are pioneering these concepts, setting the stage for a future where urban design centers on connection.

One such city is Toronto, where the Quayside project, although controversial, aimed to create a smart city designed around people, not vehicles. Similarly, Melbourne's "Future Melbourne 2026" plan focuses on sustainability, accessibility, and community connections. In Asia, Singapore's Smart Nation initiative leverages technology to improve urban living, making the city-state more connected and community-oriented.

Looking ahead, the challenge for urban designers, city planners, and policymakers is to create cities that, while embracing progress and technological advancement, also prioritize social connection, inclusivity, and community well-being. This isn't an easy task, but it's essential if we want to combat the loneliness epidemic.

Our journey through the future of urban design doesn't end here. Individuals, communities, and local governments can get involved in shaping their city's future. Remember, the power to build connected, compassionate communities lies in our hands.

In the meantime, think about your own community. How can it be improved? What steps can you take to foster connection in your neighborhood?

Your actions, no matter how small, can contribute to the wider effort to combat loneliness and build socially connected communities.

Chapter 12: Looking Forward: Wellness and Emotional Health

The Role of Wellness in Combating Loneliness

The role of wellness in combatting loneliness is a subject deserving of in-depth exploration. Wellness encompasses much more than physical health; it encompasses mental, emotional, and spiritual well-being, all integral components in mitigating feelings of loneliness and fostering social connection.

Understanding Wellness

The World Health Organization defines health not merely as the absence of disease, but as a state of complete physical, mental, and social well-being. The concept of wellness expands on this definition. It's about living a fulfilling life, characterized by good health, happiness, and a sense of purpose. It's a proactive approach to health that includes the nurturing of mental and emotional well-being, as well as physical health.

Mental Wellness and Loneliness

Loneliness is both a cause and a result of poor mental health. Chronic loneliness can lead to mental health issues like depression and anxiety, while existing mental health conditions can exacerbate feelings of loneliness.

Promoting mental wellness involves fostering positive mental health habits, including regular exercise, adequate sleep, and healthy eating. In addition, seeking professional help when needed, and practicing mindfulness and meditation can improve mental health.

Emotional Wellness: Feeling Connected

Emotional wellness revolves around acknowledging and expressing feelings, coping with challenges, and maintaining positive relationships. It is a key component in the fight against loneliness. One can foster emotional wellness by learning to manage stress effectively, practicing resilience, and developing a positive outlook.

In the context of loneliness, emotional wellness can help individuals understand and express their feelings of loneliness and seek out social connections. Furthermore, it can help individuals develop empathy and understanding, fostering deeper connections with others.

Spiritual Wellness: A Sense of Purpose and Connection

Spiritual wellness, while not tied to any specific religious belief, involves a sense of connection to something greater than oneself, providing a sense of purpose and meaning. Practices like meditation, mindfulness, and activities that inspire awe and wonder, can cultivate spiritual wellness.

In the fight against loneliness, a sense of purpose can act as a powerful motivator for connection. It can drive individuals to seek and nurture relationships, find like-minded communities, and engage in activities that promote social well-being.

The Intersection of Wellness and Social Connection

A holistic approach to wellness can help combat loneliness. Prioritizing mental and emotional health, acknowledging and addressing feelings of loneliness, fostering empathy and understanding, and finding a sense of purpose are all part of the equation.

Wellness activities such as group exercise classes, meditation groups, or community gardening can not only promote individual well-being but also provide opportunities for social connection. Similarly, digital platforms can connect individuals seeking to improve their wellness, fostering online communities that can help mitigate feelings of isolation.

As we forge ahead into a future where loneliness is an acknowledged public health concern, it's important to recognize and utilize the role of wellness in combating this epidemic. By understanding the interconnectedness of our physical, mental, emotional, and spiritual well-being, we can better equip ourselves and our communities to fight loneliness and promote lasting social connections.

Promoting Emotional Health in a Lonely Society

Loneliness can have profound impacts on a person's emotional health, leading to a sense of isolation, despair, and even depression. Hence, the question that begs an answer is, "How can we promote emotional health in a lonely society?"

Understanding Emotional Health

Emotional health refers to our ability to manage and express the emotions that arise from our experiences. It includes the capability to handle stress, to feel and acknowledge our feelings, to maintain positive relationships, and to enjoy life despite its ups and downs.

Emotionally healthy people have a certain level of resilience. They can withstand life's adversities, cope with stress, and bounce back from hardships. But emotional health does not imply the absence of negative emotions.

Instead, it involves being aware of our emotions – positive or negative – and having the ability to deal with them.

Impact of Loneliness on Emotional Health

Loneliness, if persistent, can have a detrimental impact on emotional health. It can lead to feelings of worthlessness and a heightened sense of vulnerability. Moreover, it can result in anxiety, depression, and other mental health conditions.

Promoting Emotional Health: Strategies and Solutions

Despite the prevalence of loneliness in our society, several strategies can be used to promote emotional health:

- **Self-Awareness and Expression**: Recognize and acknowledge your feelings instead of suppressing or ignoring them. It's okay to feel lonely, anxious, or stressed. Allow yourself to express these feelings in a constructive way, such as through writing, speaking with a trusted friend, or seeking professional help.
- **Mindfulness and Meditation**: These practices help anchor the mind in the present, reducing feelings of anxiety and loneliness. They improve our capacity to manage and respond to our feelings, thereby enhancing emotional health.
- **Self-Care**: Activities like physical exercise, balanced diet, and sufficient sleep contribute to overall well-being, including emotional health.

Regular exercise, in particular, has been proven to reduce symptoms of anxiety and improve mood.

- **Social Connection**: Fostering relationships and social networks can help combat loneliness and boost emotional health. This could involve reconnecting with old friends, joining social clubs or groups with similar interests, or volunteering.
- **Professional Help**: If feelings of loneliness and emotional distress persist, it may be helpful to seek professional help. Therapists and counselors are trained to help you understand and navigate your feelings and provide strategies for improving your emotional health.
- **Community Support**: On a societal level, community support can play a significant role in promoting emotional health. This could involve the provision of accessible mental health services, the promotion of mental health awareness, and the development of initiatives that foster social connection.

Promoting emotional health in a lonely society is a complex, multifaceted challenge that requires both individual and collective action. By acknowledging the power of our emotions, prioritizing self-care, fostering social connections, and advocating for community support, we can begin to build a society that is not only less lonely but also emotionally healthier.

Towards a Future of Mental Wellness and Connection

In a society increasingly grappling with issues of loneliness and isolation, creating a future where mental wellness and connection are prioritized is not only desirable but also necessary. But what does a future of mental wellness and connection look like, and how can we get there?

Visualizing the Future

In a future where mental wellness and connection are valued, we would see a society that is more empathetic, compassionate, and understanding. Mental health wouldn't be stigmatized, but instead, it would be seen as an integral part of overall health. Individuals would be equipped with the skills and knowledge to manage their mental and emotional health, and support would be easily accessible to those who need it.

In this society, connections would be nurtured. People would actively seek meaningful relationships and work to maintain them. Opportunities for social interaction and community engagement would be abundant, fostering a sense of belonging and mutual support.

Path to Mental Wellness and Connection

There's no magic formula for creating this ideal society, but there are certainly steps that we can take to move towards this vision. These include individual strategies, community initiatives, and societal shifts.

1. Promoting Self-Care

Promoting mental wellness starts with the individual. Encourage self-care activities, such as regular physical exercise, balanced diet, and adequate sleep. Mindfulness and meditation can also be powerful tools for managing stress and enhancing emotional awareness.

2. Encouraging Emotional Literacy

Equip individuals with the skills to recognize, understand, and manage their emotions. This can be done through educational programs in schools, workshops in workplaces, or accessible online resources. Emotional literacy can help individuals navigate their own emotions and empathize with others, promoting both mental wellness and social connection.

3. Fostering Resilience

Resilience is the ability to bounce back from adversity. Foster resilience by promoting coping strategies, such as positive thinking, problem-solving, and stress management. Encouraging a growth mindset, the belief that abilities and intelligence can be developed through effort and perseverance, can also help individuals overcome challenges and foster mental wellness.

4. Cultivating Social Connections

Encourage people to foster meaningful relationships. This could involve creating opportunities for social interaction, promoting activities that foster community engagement, or offering platforms for people to connect over shared interests.

5. Creating Supportive Environments

Create environments that support mental wellness and social connection. This could involve designing schools and workplaces that promote interaction and collaboration, developing urban spaces that encourage community engagement, or creating digital platforms that facilitate meaningful connections.

6. Advocating for Mental Health

Advocate for policies and initiatives that promote mental health and social connection. This could involve campaigning for increased funding for mental health services, advocating for mental health education in schools, or pushing for policies that foster community connection.

7. Utilizing Technology

Leverage technology to promote mental wellness and connection. Digital platforms can offer accessible resources for mental health support, as well as opportunities for social connection.

8. Destigmatizing Mental Health

Work to destigmatize mental health. This involves raising awareness about mental health issues, promoting understanding and empathy, and challenging negative stereotypes and misconceptions.

Creating a future of mental wellness and connection may be a challenging task, but it's an essential one. By taking individual, community, and societal steps, we can move towards a society that values mental wellness and fosters connection. It's a future worth working for.

Conclusion: The Future of Loneliness and Human Connection

As we reach the end of our journey through the complex web of loneliness and its implications for our society, it's time to look ahead to the future, with all its challenges and opportunities. What might the future of loneliness and human connection look like? What steps can we take individually and collectively to mitigate the loneliness epidemic and foster a more connected, compassionate society? These are critical questions to ponder as we move forward.

The Future Landscape

In an increasingly digital age, the face of loneliness and human connection is changing. While technology can connect us with others across the globe in an instant, it cannot replace the depth and richness of face-to-face interactions. As we become more intertwined with our digital tools, we must strive to strike a balance, leveraging technology to augment, not replace, our innate need for human connection.

Simultaneously, demographic trends, such as an aging population, increased urbanization, and changing family structures, will likely continue to influence the prevalence of loneliness. We must adapt our strategies and interventions to address these evolving challenges.

Towards an Empathetic and Connected Society

The antidote to loneliness lies not only in individual actions but also in creating an empathetic and connected society. A society that values mental health as much as physical health, that educates its citizens about the importance of social connections, that fosters community engagement, and that provides robust support systems for those struggling with loneliness.

This involves several key steps:

1. Mental Health Education: This is not just about raising awareness but also about equipping individuals with practical skills to manage their emotional health and foster strong social connections.

2. Community Building: Develop community initiatives that promote interaction and engagement, such as community centers, shared spaces, and group activities. These serve as platforms for building relationships and fostering a sense of belonging.

3. Leveraging Technology for Good: Use technology to connect people in meaningful ways, providing platforms for shared experiences, mutual support, and community engagement. But remember, technology should complement, not replace, face-to-face interaction.

4. Policy Changes: Advocate for policies that recognize and address the loneliness epidemic, such as increased funding for mental health services, policies to foster community connections, and workplace policies that promote work-life balance.

5. Research and Innovation: Continue to invest in research to better understand the complexities of loneliness and develop innovative solutions. This is an evolving field, and we must continue to learn and adapt.

An Individual Journey

While societal efforts are critical, combating loneliness also requires individual action. Each of us has a role to play in fostering our own mental wellness and cultivating our social connections.

We can take steps to nurture our emotional health, such as practicing mindfulness, seeking professional help when needed, and taking time for self-care. We can also make efforts to connect with others, reaching out to loved ones, making new connections, and participating in community activities.

A Note of Hope

The loneliness epidemic may seem like an insurmountable challenge, but it's important to remember that every challenge presents an opportunity for growth and innovation. Loneliness is a complex issue, but it's one that we can overcome. As we move forward, let's carry with us a sense of hope and determination.

With understanding, empathy, and concerted action, we can combat the loneliness epidemic and build a future characterized by mental wellness and deep, fulfilling human connections. We're all in this together, and together, we can make a difference.

As you close this book, remember that the end of a chapter can be the beginning of a new journey. The conversation about loneliness and human connection doesn't end here; it's an ongoing dialogue that requires our collective attention and effort.

I sincerely hope that this book has offered you valuable insights and practical strategies that you can use to contribute to this important cause.

Together, let's move towards a future where loneliness is understood, addressed, and ultimately, overcome.

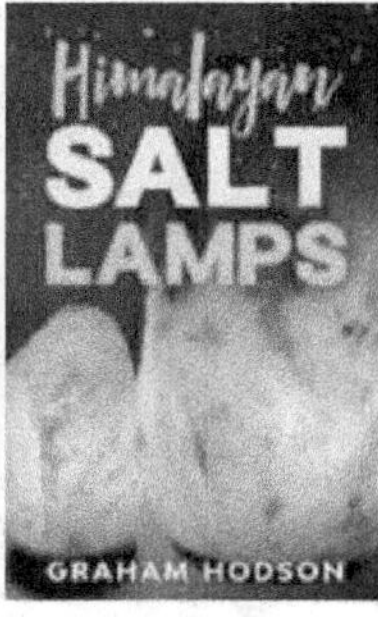

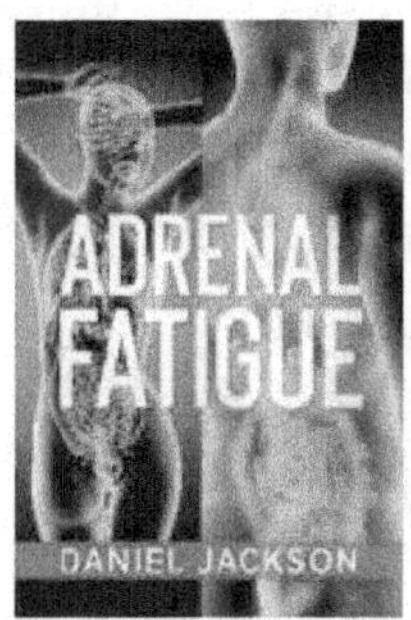

Take a look at more great books available from Rockwood Publishing

... some for FREE!

Just visit the link below:

rockwoodpublishing.co.uk

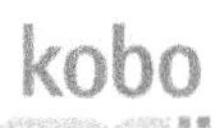

to the subject matter covered. The information included in this book has been compiled to give an overview of the subject(s) and detail some of the symptoms, treatments etc. that are available to people with this condition. It is not intended to give medical advice. For a firm diagnosis of your condition, and for a treatment plan suitable for you, you should consult your doctor or consultant. The writer of this book and the publisher are not responsible for any damages or negative consequences following any of the treatments or methods highlighted in this book. Website links are for informational purposes and should not be seen as a personal endorsement; the same applies to the products detailed in this book. The reader should also be aware that although the web links included were correct at the time of writing, they may become out of date in the future.

Disclaimers

The content contained within this book is for information and entertainment purposes only, and in no way purports to represent professional medical opinion. It should NOT be used as a substitute for expert advice, and you must consult with your designated health professional before acting upon any information contained herein or before undertaking any practice whose methodology is referred to in this book. The author is NOT a registered health professional and the text merely represents personal opinion, not medical fact. The author cannot be held responsible for the consequences of any action derived from the reading of this book, as the content is not based on diagnosis and subsequent regimen. It is the reader's responsibility to seek proper, professional medical advice from a registered health practitioner in connection with any material contained within this book.

Legal Disclaimer (part 1)

Nothing in this book should be construed as an attempt to diagnose, treat or cure. The information in this book is intended to be a community resource. The author takes no responsibility for any informational material or brochures produced using information

taken from this book. The author has endeavoured to ensure that all information is correct at the time of publication. This information, however, is subject to change without notice. The author makes no warranty with regard to the accuracy of any information and will not be liable for any errors or omissions. Any liability that arises as a result of this information is hereby excluded to the fullest extent allowed by law.
This information should not be used as a substitute for seeking independent professional advice.

Legal Disclaimer (part 2)

Disclaimer and Terms of Use:

a) i. In publishing this information, the author makes no representations concerning the efficacy, appropriateness or suitability of any products or treatments. Use this information at your own risk. The compiler is not a doctor and has no medical background or training.

ii. Statements and information regarding dietary supplements, books and any products mentioned have not been evaluated by any health authority and are not intended to diagnose, treat, cure or prevent any disease or health condition.

b) In view of the possibility of human error, neither the author nor any other party involved in providing this information, warrant that the information contained therein is in every respect accurate or complete and they are not responsible nor liable for any errors or omissions that may be found or for the results obtained from the use of such information. The entire risk as to use of this information is assumed by the user.

c) You are encouraged to consult other sources and confirm the information.

d) The information you access is provided "as is". No warranty, expressed or implied, is given as to the accuracy, completeness or timeliness of any information herein, or for obtaining legal advice. To the fullest extent permissible pursuant to applicable law, neither the author nor any other parties who have been involved in the creation, preparation, printing, or delivering of this information assume responsibility for the completeness, accuracy, timeliness, errors or omissions of said information and assume no liability for any direct, incidental, consequential, indirect, or punitive damages as well as any circumstance for any complication, injuries, side effects or other medical accidents to person or property arising from or in connection with the use or reliance upon any information contained herein.

e) The author is not responsible for the contents of any linked site or any link contained in a linked site, or any changes or update to such sites. The inclusion of any link does not imply endorsement by the author. The author makes no representations or claims as to the quality, content and accuracy of the information, services, products, messages which may be provided by such resources, and specifically disclaims any warranties, including but not limited to implied or express warranties of merchantability or fitness for any particular usage, application or purpose.

f) The information provided is general in nature and is intended for educational and informational purposes only. It is not intended to replace or substitute the evaluation, judgment, diagnosis, and medical or preventative care of a physician, paediatrician, therapist and/or health care provider.

g) Any medical, nutritional, dietetic, therapeutic or other decisions, dosages, treatments or drug regimes should be made in consultation with a health care practitioner. Do not discontinue treatment or medication without first consulting your physician, clinician or therapist.

h) By reading this information, you signify your assent to these terms and conditions of use. If you do not agree to these terms and conditions of use, do not read/use this information. If any provision of these terms and conditions of use shall be determined to be unlawful, void or for any reason unenforceable, then that provision shall be deemed severable from this agreement and shall not affect the validity and enforceability of any remaining provisions.

i) The information, services, products, messages and other materials, individually and collectively, are provided with the understanding that the author is not engaged in rendering medical advice or recommendations.

j) The information and the terms of use are subject to change without notice. The material provided as is without warranty of any kind and may include inaccuracies and/or typographical errors. The author makes no representations about the suitability of this information for any purpose. The author disclaims all warranties with regard to this information, including all implied warranties, and in no event shall the author be held liable, resulting from, or in any way related to, the use of this information.

k) The unauthorized alteration of the content of this information is expressly prohibited. The author, its agents and representatives shall not be responsible for any claims, actions or damages which may arise on account of the unauthorized alteration of this information.

www.ingramcontent.com/pod-product-compliance
Lightning Source LLC
Chambersburg PA
CBHW050512160726
48003CB00001B/272